WALLASEY AT WAR
including MORETON

CONTENTS

Published for Wallasey Historical Society by
Ian & Marilyn Boumphrey
Design & Origination
Ian Boumphrey – Desk Top Publisher
The Nook Acrefield Road Prenton Wirral CH42 8LD
email: ian@yesterdayswirral.co.uk
Printed by
Eaton Press Direct Westfield Road Wallasey CH44 7JB

ISBN 1-899241-14-0

£6.95

INTRODUCTION

Those who lived in Wallasey throughout the "Blitz", whether they were at school, in the Home Guard, the Fire Services, the Wardens, whether they were housewives, shopkeepers, nurses, or those in other occupations, all usually had tales to tell of amazing escapes or tragic incidents. The personal memories of those momentous times of 1940 and 1941 should be recorded in the annals of local history 60 years on. This book, produced by The Wallasey Historical Society, goes some way towards recording some of those events. But it is only a droplet from this ocean of memories.

With the reproduction of the "Warden's Service" book, now out of print, statistics from contemporary newspapers and records, this Society has endeavoured to produce a record available to all. A comprehensive index assists in searching for information and names.

The publication was inspired by a Community Grant from New Wallasey for a Millennium project. The book was originally intended to be a collection of various articles by members, however, one of these pieces submitted has inspired the theme "Wallasey at War."

It was felt that this book should be produced before it was too late. We all forget details, people move away, people pass on, taking with them memories rich in history.

The Wallasey Historical Society hopes that you will enjoy this book.

SUBSCRIBERS

Mrs. S. Abbott
Mr. D. Annison
Mrs. D. Avery
Mr. V.N. Barwick
Miss. M. Bell
Mr. J.R. & Mrs. M.P. Bird
Mrs. J. Boughey
Mr. I.G. Boumphrey
Mrs. M.D. Boumphrey
Mrs. M.J. Carlisle
Mrs. M. Christey
Mrs. M.E. Clare
Mrs. S.J. Collinson
Mrs. G. Collinson Stokes
Mrs. E. Curran
Mr. P.J. Curran
Mrs. D. D'arcy
Miss. S. Davies
Mrs. J. Done
Mr. G. Dooley
Mrs. M. Doughty
Mrs. P.J. Dunn
Mrs. P. Eccleson
Mr. T. Edgar
Mr. K.F.& Mrs. J. Edwards
Mrs. B. Evans
Mr. E.F. Godfrey
Mr. J.T. & Mrs. S. Hodson
Mr. R.G. Hall
Mrs. A. Harwood
Mrs. B. Harwood
Mr. B. Higgins
Mrs. J. Hockey
Mr. P. Hockey

Mrs. P. Hoppins
Hoylake Historical Society
Mrs. K. Humphries
Mrs. J. James
Mr. & Mrs. R.P. Jamieson
Miss. N.B. Jones
Mr. & Mrs. R.H. Jones
Miss. S.E. Jones
Mrs. E.M. Keegan
Mrs. A. Lakin
Mrs. M. Lancaster
Mrs. F. Langshaw
Dr. R. Lawrence
Mr. E. Lennie
Mr. R.E. Lewis
Mrs. H.M. Longster
Miss. M.T. Lynch
Mr. F. McEneany
Mrs. E.B. Miller
Mrs. J. Morris
Mr. H. Nickson
Miss. E.F. Nielson
Mr. A.P. Nute
Mrs. O.G. O'Donnell
Mrs. J. O'Sullivan
Miss. R.A. Ogden
Mrs. I. Owens
Mrs. B.J. Parkinson
Mrs. A. Parry
Mrs. M. Pemberton
Mrs. B.M. Perry
Mr. G.S. Rebecca
Mr. J.S. Rebecca
Mrs. B. Reid

Mrs. B. Rhodes
Dr. P.S. Richards
Mr. & Mrs. M. Roberts
Mr. K. H. Robinson
Mrs. M. Ryan
Mrs. G. & Mr. J. Saville
Mrs. J.M. Schofield
Mrs. A. Slater
Mr. N.E. Smith
Mrs. P.M. Snowden
Mr. & Mrs. C. Spiers
Mr. J. Stevenson
Mrs. C. Stonall
Mr. & Mrs. J.E. & H.M. Sumner
Mrs. C. Swanson
Mrs. A.E. Tanner
Mr. D.F. Taylor
Mrs. P.R. Thompson
Mr. B. A. Thomson
Mrs. J. Thomson
Miss. A.K. Treleaven
Mr. B. Wagstaff
Mrs. V. Ward
Mr. J. Wealthy
Mrs. B.R. Whiteway
Mr. & Mrs. K.E. Wilcoxon
Mr. & Mrs. J. & I. Wilson
Mr. & Mrs. D. Williams
Mrs. G. Williams
Mr. & Mrs. E. Winstanley
Mr. & Mrs. H. Wolfe
Mr. D.D. Young

This is the cover of the Wallasey Warden Service 1938 – 1944 which was published for the Wallasey Warden Service and from which the following 30 pages have been reproduced. Additional information has been added to the "Chronological Summary of Raids on Wallasey" – section of the booklet – details of which were not available at the time the publication was printed in 1944. A few other minor alterations have been made to the text but the main body of it has been left in its original form. Photographs taken at the time have also been included.

ACKNOWLEDGEMENTS

The Wallasey Historical Society would like to thank all those people who have helped in any way to make this publication possible. We are particularly grateful to the following:- Basil Thomson for the inspiration; Society contributors for their memories; Society proof readers for their patience; Jenny Done, Reference Librarian, Wallasey Central Library, for help and support with records and photographs; John Hankey and Phyllis Snowden for dealing with finances; Ian Boumphrey for his enthusiasm and devotion, and compiling the index; Keith Edwards for classifying the list of subscribers; Eric Lowe, Superintendant Wallasey Police (retired), for loan of records and photographs; to Joy Hockey for the idea and pursuing the grant; to all the Subscribers for their financial support and to "New Wallasey" for a Community Grant.

Foreword

By His Worship The Mayor of Wallasey
Alderman John Pennington, J.P.

"Yet now I do not repent me of all trouble I have been at to arrive where I am."

Mr. Valiant

I have just finished reading two remarkable books by Arthur Bryant — "The Years of Endurance" and "The Years of Victory." These books are a record of the valour, tenacity, patience and sacrifices of the British people during the long years they fought and defeated one of the greatest of the warriors, administrators, and soldiers of the ages—Napoleon. The struggle lasted from 1793 to 1815 and during that time, apart from the uneasy truce called the Treaty of Amiens, our people, often without allies and quite alone, defied the dictator and emerged victorious. Remembering Pitt's immortal words—They had saved Europe by their example and themselves by their exertions.

In September, 1939, history repeated itself, and the call came again to the British people to resist a dictator who menaced their liberties and the peace of the world. The old Saxon battle order rang through the land— "Close ranks' — "Stand Fast." No Service responded to this call more devotedly than the men, women and young people comprising the Civil Defence Services of Britain. A great number throughout the country had been fitting themselves for the task for some years. At a time when many scoffed (or affected to scoff) at the possibility of war and feigned to be sceptical of the possibility of air warfare, men and women and young people responded to the urgent call to equip themselves with the knowledge to serve their country.

When the time came they were ready. All branches of the C.D. Services excelled themselves in devotion to their duty. Air warfare was new. Its terrible and devastating effects could only be guessed at. Reports from the Spanish Civil War helped a little and had been closely studied. The lessons of Guernica and other Spanish cities and towns had not been lost, but they were not widely known. No praise is too high to give to the instructors and lecturers who trained and prepared the volunteers for all branches of the work. During the period of waiting— the 'phoney war,' as it was called—the Services stood to and did not relax. They perfected themselves by all the means at their disposal to master every phase of their job and they went into action with a courage and a self-sacrifice which earned the gratitude of the country and the admiration of the world.

No one will begrudge a special word of praise for all those in Wallasey (including the women and young people) who from August, 1940, to November, 1941, especially during the dreadful nights of December, 1940 and March and May, 1941, played their part with such valour, steadiness and competence. The form of attack was new and terrifying. Losses were great and casualties heavy. There was no flinching amongst those who had responded to the need of the nation.

The members of the Civil Defence Services had set their feet on the path of duty, and they followed that path through all the trials, sufferings and sacrifices demanded by the cause of Liberty and Freedom for which they fought.

History will record that not the least of the reasons for Hitler's failure to dominate Europe and the world was the staunch and fearless conduct of the Civil Defence Services. They were worthy of all that is best in their country's long and honourable history.

The war is not over and the period of waiting calls for patience and forbearance. But victory is sure and certain. When it comes every member of the Civil Defence Services who had fought the good fight and kept faith with the country will, in the peace of after years, be able to say with a quiet pride the words which head this "Foreword." There are those who have no memorial save that which we have in our hearts remembering them.

Wallasey is grateful to all. I offer every member of the Civil Defence Services a most respectful Salute.

(signed) JOHN PENNINGTON
Mayor.

WHEN WAR BECAME A GRIM REALITY

❊

The following foreward is by
Mr. JOHN ORMEROD, O.B.E.,
CHIEF CONSTABLE,
A.R.P. CONTROLLER,
COUNTY BOROUGH OF WALLASEY.

❊

This record is devoted to the Warden Service, a branch of Civil Defence on which I had largely to depend for my first information. These men and women trained and equipped themselves in the early days of 1939 for the many tasks which then lay ahead.

When the grim reality of war visited this Borough, pouring from the skies the worst that the German Air Force could inflict, we found this determined body of loyal citizens accepting indescribable hardships, and facing imminent danger of death, With no other thought than that their duty had to be completed,

They fought the fires, cheered the stricken, and in so many ways assisted those in distress.

Many unfortunate citizens will long remember the helping hand proffered to them by a tired, begrimed Warden amongst the wreckage of their homes.

The Wardens' courage and devotion to duty has never been questioned; much of their work may be forgotten.

This document may serve to revive the flagging memories.

Message from The Chief Warden

Mr. J. Reginald Smith

This record of the Warden Service of the Borough of Wallasey has been compiled so that the members of that Service and the Public generally will have a reminder of the days from early in 1938 until the end of 1944 by which time it was hoped that the worst was over.

It has been prepared by our friend, Mr. George Proudman. I know the amount of work which was involved in extracting and collating the mass of detail, and our thanks are due to him for undertaking this task.

If reading this causes you to throw your mind back to those dark times of 1940/41 – recalling the happenings in your Sectors and Groups – and causes you to say "Never again shall this happen," then I think this record will have served its purpose.

I am glad of this opportunity of putting on record my admiration of the men and women of the Wallasey Warden Service, who so valiantly carried out their jobs through enemy attacks. It has been a source of pride and pleasure to me to have served as their Chief Warden, and my task has been lightened by the wonderful help and loyal co-operation I have always received from my deputy, Mr George Proudman – it was his ready assistance which enabled me to carry on at all times. My thanks and appreciation are also due in no small measure to my Head Wardens and their Deputies, my office staff, and the members of the Service in general.

Royal visit to Wallasey 6 November 1940.
Their Majesties speaking to the Deputy Head Warden outside Wallasey Town Hall

Introducing the Service

On the map of England there is a geographical feature that is easily identified – the Wirral Peninsula. On the north-eastern tip of that Peninsula lies the Borough of Wallasey and it is, as the map shows, the part of the Peninsula that lies nearest to the Gladstone Docks, the most modern of the Mersey's dock system and, to the south it is bounded by Birkenhead docks.

It is not material to this account to attempt to decide whether when the enemy hit the Borough they were aiming at it or were just making singularly inaccurate attempts to hit the docks and/or lay mines in the river, but the fact remains that they did drop numerous bombs on to the residential area which Wallasey mainly comprises. Those who went through the war as members of the Warden Service were and are grateful that they were introduced to ordeal by bombing in stages – never at the time appearing to be easy but subsequently judged to be nothing compared with what followed.

The Service had been adequately prepared before the war and, when the time came in September, 1939, organised itself on a war-time footing. For a time its activities closely resembled those of pre-war practices, never divested of humour, lectures, post duty, enforcement of blackout restrictions and . . . . the inevitable darts. After a brief period of tension, even the air raid warnings – verbally of so many colours for easy telephonic identification – ceased to have their first sense of urgency and so things went on until, after the Battle of Britain, the sirens began to sound in earnest. Air activity in those days can be summed up in two words – minelaying (by the enemy) and splinters (from our guns). For a period the main danger which Wardens ran was from our own A.A. gunfire yet, despite its apparent propinquity on many occasions, it has not, to the writer's knowledge, been recorded that any Warden received a direct hit on his helmet from even a small piece of one of our own shells.

These were essentially the days of practical preparation and they were accepted and utilised as such. Came the first enemy bombs on Wallasey and the Warden Service was soon in action.

A chronological record is given elsewhere of what took place but the Borough was subjected in greater or less measure, to high-explosive bombs, including those of the delayed action variety, parachute mining, and incendiaries of different types.

Rest centres proved their great value in Wallasey as elsewhere, and thither it was frequently necessary for Wardens to escort both during air raids and after the "raiders passed" sirens, convoys of bombed-out people and, high though their appreciation grew to be of the services of the Wardens, it was no greater than the Wardens' praise for the courage and cheerfulness of residents in such depressing conditions with homes and household goods damaged if not destroyed, themselves evicted with their lives admittedly, but dirty always, and often inadequately clothed. One remembers a naval officer with filthy face and hands, wearing pyjamas, service coat and, lest he be improperly dressed, service cap who on his way to and in the Rest Centre, kept his companions in the best of spirits. No words, it may be added, would do more than justice to those who were responsible for the running of the Rest Centres.

To supplement this brief introduction. Councillor J. H. Wensley, J.P. who has been throughout very closely associated with Civil Defence, has written the following on the early days of air raids precautions-

In March, 1937, I had the honour to be appointed Chairman of the new!y-formed A.R.P. Committee. We soon found ourselves confronted with a multitude of problems, all connected with the protection and well-being of the civil population in the event of war. Many of the original plans were the product of individual imagination, but, even in those early days, with the prospect of war considered as only a remote possibility, they were tested, developed and completed.

My Committee, the chief officials, and the Chief Constable (who drafted the A.R.P. scheme), helped and supported me with a vigour, skill, and competence which I shall always recall with gratitude.

The framework of the organisation was taking shape; machinery slowly but surely set into motion. As volunteers received their training, and were allocated to their various tasks, it became clear that the tireless planning of many months, together with the growing spirit of the volunteers, had created a defensive force which, if called into action, would go far to assure the maximum of protection, skilled treatment for the injured, and help and comfort for the distressed, always providing that the courage and determination of the Civil Defence workers could stand the test.

Of that we had little doubt. How, in the event, these gallant members faced the concentrated horrors rained on our townspeople from the skies, how they recovered the dead, cared for the wounded, succoured the injured, forms the basis of this chronicle.

Since the inception of A.R.P. to the present day. I am proud and privileged to have been so closely associated with such a fine body of our citizens, who have shown in the highest degree those imperishable qualities of courage, dauntless valour, steadfastness, and outstanding resource.

The original conception was that the Warden Service should be a voluntary organisation, the duties of which would be carried out by responsible and reliable members of the public, who would undertake to advise and help their fellow citizens in all the risks and calamities which might follow from air attack.

On the outbreak of war, a number of the Wardens were appointed on a whole-time basis, but as time went on, and the war intensified, greater demands on National resources were made. Calls were made for greater sacrifices of leisure and convenience from all volunteers, and further claims upon available man power entailed considerable reductions in the number of whole-time personnel from time to time.

This meant re-organisation and adjustment of ideas, with closer co-operation and assistance from the whole of the personnel to ensure that the efficiency of the Service and the adequate protection of the civil population were not impaired.

The value of the Service lay in the fact that it had a very intimate connection with the general public. The issuing of respirators and their fitting and periodical inspection; the numerous house to house calls on the census returns of Communal, Anderson and Morrison Shelters; the Gas Cleansing Scheme in private houses; the formation and the training of the Fire Guard; the lighting patrol, and the watchful stand-by duty, kept us in close touch in the early days.

Yet not at first were they welcomed. The Wardens were considered little more than a nuisance at that time, but by their high sense of duty, untiring energy, tact, and personality, they gradually built up a bond of friendship which was the keystone of their success and gained them the goodwill and confidence of the public.

During the raids this bond of friendship was further strengthened by the friendly tap on the door to enquire if "all's well," a peep into the shelter, a cheery word, and the sound of the measured beat of the hob-nailed boots passing leisurely by—just a Warden on patrol.

The people of Wallasey found discipline in their Warden Service. Though not an armed force, the Wardens showed when occasion demanded, the essential characteristics of a disciplined body. They took episode after episode in their stride, turning out to every raid irrespective of tour of duty, for numbers were so few that it meant everyone was required on duty.

In the ranks of the Service were several members of the Town Council, including our Member of Parliament, who found time to take up active Civil Defence work in addition to their many other public duties. Many of the men in the ranks had seen long service in the Army, as their decorations showed. Ex-Navy and Mercantile Marine men (the gallant seventies) retired from the sea, willing and not too old to serve on the land, joined the Service.

During the raids there were so many instances of devotion to duty and so many brave deeds that it is impossible to record them all or mention individual names in this record. Although they escaped official recognition they will live long in the memory of those who witnessed them and the measure of the work accomplished is indicated in the following extracts from reports, which are representative of many others: "Very heavy bombs in — Drive. Houses demolished on top of shelters. After difficulty extracted mother and baby. Worked through to next door, girl injured, unconscious. Warden — squeezes in and helps to lift and push out to Warden —; still alive when rescued, carried to shelter. More to get out, girl with damaged shoulder, very difficult to get out owing to pain and not able to help herself. Out at last and carried to safety with her young brother, both suffering from shock."

"Call for assistance from — Street."

"People buried under debris, house on fire. Turned off gas and electric; got people out after a spot of bother. Delayed action bomb lower down the street, people removed to safety. Women Wardens worked like Trojans providing hot drinks and comforts for the old people. First-aid work good. First-aid man and driver arrived, packed van with casualties. Police arrived — explained position to them and handed over."

"At one incident Wardens remained constantly on duty for 48 hours, during which time they attended to 18 H.E. incidents, rescuing many people from debris, organised fire parties which successfully dealt with over 50 houses on which incendiaries had fallen."

"Then again an injured Warden volunteers to stand by and direct services. Another H.E. drops, causing shock and further injuries, yet she volunteers to lead the Police to — carrying blankets, and works throughout the night rendering first aid."

"Another Warden, very seriously injured, insists on his comrade being attended to first as he says he is badly hurt, and when he is being taken away in the ambulance, asks for someone to be sent to — Road as the people need help there, and to look after his Sector."

"These Wardens never had a thought for themselves, and right throughout the service the care of the public was their chief concern, and these cases must suffice for the many that took place nightly throughout the Borough during the raids."

Merseyside's Part in The Battle of Britain

The first bomb fell in the Orkneys on October 17th, 1939, and it was in the Orkneys that the first civilian was killed on March 16th, 1940. The first bomb to fall on the mainland was near Canterbury on May 9th, 1940.

It was not until after the surrender of the French in June, 1940, that the German Air Force started its attack proper by sending bombers on Britain in large numbers and the Battle of Britain began.

For some months London and the South bore the full weight of the attack; the Luftwaffe thought to vanquish the City by a knockout blow, but it was repulsed. With the fall of France the attack was reorganised from occupied territory. Attention was diverted from London to the industrial centres in the provinces; Middlesbrough, Coventry, Bristol, Birmingham, Sheffield and other cities were visited with devastating effect. With improved night practice, coast reconnaissance and navigation the enemy plotted a pathway through the sky via Bristol up the Welsh border and found his way to Merseyside.

The air raid alarm, the sound of which we all came to dislike so much, sounded for the first time in the Merseyside area on June 25th, 1940, when enemy planes were heard in the air, and the first bombs fell on the night of July 28/29th, near a searchlight post at Altcar, and in the open country about Irby, Thurstaston and Neston, without doing serious damage.

On the night of August 10th, 1940, the night after a raid on Birkenhead, the first bombs fell on Wallasey when property was damaged, four people were killed and four seriously injured with many slighter casualties, and our long months of ordeal commenced, widening monthly until May the following year.

Aided by the waters and the River Mersey glistening in the moonlight the Luftwaffe's marksmen visited us time and again, dropping their loads of incendiaries to light a beacon target for the high explosive bombs carried by heavier aircraft following on. Raids on the industrial areas, the docks, and the residential areas on which thousands of incendiaries were dropped were an attempt to obliterate the whole of our area and break the spirit of the inhabitants, and strike at the nerve and courage of the civilians by disorganising their daily lives. He did the latter but the former. No!

QUIZ COMPETITION

To maintain enthusiasm and efficiency, which reached their highest pitch during periods of enemy activity but were apt to decline when it was only a matter of carrying out routine work, the Chief Warden instituted a Quiz Competition in 1943 and presented a shield. Teams of seven a side represented the different Groups, instructors being excluded and the competition was well supported, there being good attendances of Wardens at the contests in each round. The questions were put by Inspector Williams, and the competition was decided on the knock-out principle. Ultimately the two following teams met in the final after some very close results in the earlier Stages:-

Groups 10/11, Moreton. - Mr. J. Mitchell (Capt.), Mr. D. L. Walker, Mrs. S. Heaney, Mr. P. Cross, Mrs. H. Lloyd, Mr. E. R. Haws, and Mr. G. Smith.

Group 2. (runners-up). - Mr. G. Askham (Capt.), Mr. H. Massey, Mr. E. Woodcock, Mr. H. W. J. Beak, Miss O. Attwell-Smith, Mr. F. Saunders, and Mr. J. Wilde.

After a most exciting contest the Moreton team won by 93 points to 88 points and the shield remains in their keeping.

Roll of Honour

**Members of the County Borough of Wallasey Warden
Service who made the Supreme Sacrifice.**

In remembrance of those who died for their Country during 1940-41.

Goodson, L.W. ...	Dec. 20th	1940	Group 5.
Rae, W.C. ...	Mar. 12th	1941	Group 5.
Thomas, G.E.L. ...	Mar. 12th	1941	Group 6.
Armstrong, P. ...	Mar. 13/14th	1941	Group 9.
Grisdale, W.W. ...	Mar. 13/14th	1941	Group 9.
Sheridan, Miss C.R.	Mar. 13/14th	1941	Group 9.
Thorpe, H. ...	Mar. 13/14th	1941	Group 9.
Whitehouse, F. ...	Mar. 13/14th	1941	Group 9.
Thompson, W.A.	Mar. 13/14th	1941	Group 2.
Jefferson, J. ...	Mar. 13/14th	1941	Group 5.
Smyth, W.J. ...	June. 1st	1941	Group 1.
McQuone, J.J. ...	Dec. 28th	1941	Group 8.

**GREATER LOVE HATH NO MAN THAN THIS THAT HE LAY
DOWN HIS LIFE FOR HIS FRIENDS.**

No words in cold print can express the great sorrow and irreparable loss
suffered by the passing of so many of our number who made the Supreme
Sacrifice. That they laid down their lives in the service of their fellow-men
and their Country, is the greatest tribute with which we can honour them.

WALLASEY'S 320 DEAD.

STATISTICS.

Official figures of Wallasey's victims during the whole of the "blitz" period

- Killed ... ... 320.
  Seriously Injured ... ... 275.
  Slightly Injured ... ... 628.

  Number of Alerts ... ... 509.
  Incidents Reported ... ... 1,044.
  H.E. Bombs in Area of Borough ... ... 641.
  Oil Bombs ... ... 8.
  Para. Mines ... ... 17.
  Number of Houses Completely Demolished ... 1,150.
  Do. Damaged ... ... 17,006.

- For a full list of the civilians that were killed in Wallasey during 1940-41 see pages 37 to 45

Chronological Summary of Raids on Wallasey

1940, AUGUST.

Raid No. 1, 1940

It was on the evening of **August 10th** that Wallasey felt the real effect of air raids for the first time. High explosive bombs fell in many parts of the Borough:– 2,3,5&7 Adelaide Street; 37/39 Cliff Road; East Street; Field Road; Florence Cottages; Gorsey Lane and Ingleby Roads; 148/150 Mill Lane; Stroude's Corner; Rake Lane; 1,3,5,6,7,8, 10 &11 Palatine Road; St. George's Mount (Belmont); 4, 6 & 8 Linwood Road; 181 Wheatland Lane; 46 Grosvenor Street; 4 & 6 Lily Grove; and 1 Tulip Grove. They fell upon streets and houses, gas and water mains, and a railway embankment. In all, there were 32 casualties, and considerable damage was done to property.

After this raid, the Chief Constable, A.R.P. Controller, sent the following message to the Chief Warden:—

Now that sufficient time has elapsed from the date of the recent unfortunate air raid to form a true estimate of the work of the Warden Service, I should like to express to you and to every individual Warden my grateful thanks for the splendid service rendered to the community.

Many have wondered ... how an entirely new service would function when the emergency arose. The Wardens have provided a most fitting and heartening answer.

It is a source of pride to me to be privileged to control such a service, and to look forward, confident that the Wardens will stand up to any demand made upon them

Raid No. 2, 1940

On the night of **August 30/31st** between 22.30 & 2.50 hrs. Wallasey received most of the bombs that fell on Merseyside. H.E. High calibre and 1 Kilo Electron type Incendiary Bombs were used. There were a few casualties, and damage was done to property in Greenwood Lane; 6 Byerley Street; 24-30 Elleray Park Road; 116 Earlston Road; 4a Bell Road; 115-159 Mount Pleasant Road, where the Wallasey High School was damaged; 22 Shakespeare Road and 15-21 & 22-26 Stoneby Drive. Unexploded bombs also fell in Rake Lane Cemetery & Elleray Park.

Raid No. 3, 1940

Considerable damage was done to property on the night of **August 31st/September 1st** when H.E. medium calibre bombs fell causing damage to:- 24/26 Littledale Road (two females injured); Town Hall & 125 Brighton Street (one female killed, one male & two females injured); 55 Bell Road; 3/4 River View (one male killed and one male & one female injured); 28 Church Street; and 2/4 Falkland Road. The south-western corner of the Town Hall received a direct hit, causing considerable damage to the organ and concert hall. Several bombs fell on the foreshore, and on the flour mills in Dock Road.

There were several casualties, and a considerable number of people had to be evacuated.

This was the first time that Group 5 had been in action proper, and their work merited the highest praise. There was some fine rescue work regardless of danger from buildings likely to fall. The co-operation of the Wardens of Groups 5 and 6 was a feature deserving special mention, as was the work of all the other Services.

Children outside Nos 9/11 Palatine Road following the first raid on Wallasey on 10 August 1940. The windows and doors of both houses have been blown out and the numbers of the houses chalked on the walls

*Crater in Brighton Street,
31 August 1940.
From left in Brighton Street
(opposite the Town Hall):-
125 - Brotherton & Co, Grocers
127 - Morris Evans, Tobacconist
129 -Kennedy & Evans, Chemist
131/133 - Brighton Hotel
        then Buchanan Road*

1940, SEPTEMBER.
Raid No. 4, 1940
On the night of **September 5/6th,** H.E. bombs of a low calibre and incendiaries were used on a raid which again took place in the Seacombe area, and resulted in damage to Vernons' Field; 57/59 Palermo Street (one man slightly injured); Kelvin Road; the Gandy Belt Works; Dock Road; Gorsey Lane and the Cheshire Lines' goods yard.

Raid No. 5, 1940
No records to show details or damage.

Raid No. 6, 1940
On September 11th, damage was confined to the Moreton area, when the Moreton Rally Centre was hit by a 50 Kg. bomb. Upton Road; Kingsmead Road; the rear of the Farmer's Arms; were damaged by bombs which also fell in the open fields round the River Birket, and the railway. There were several UXBs. Fortunately there were no casualties.

After visiting these incidents, it was easy to realise the difficulties with which the Wardens were confronted, and properly to appreciate their work. Again there was excellent co-operation with the Police which now had become a marked feature of operations.

About 100 kilo Electron Incendiaries fell in fields at rear of Meadowside and land between Reeds Lane and Fender Lane. There were also seven unexploded bombs.

Raid No. 7, 1940
On September 22nd, H.E. very heavy calibre bombs, of which two were delayed action type, fell in the area of Group 6, doing damage to 29/ 31 Lily Grove (three females killed); 28/32 Briardale Road (two males & two females killed and two males slightly injured); Alfred Road near Great Float Hotel; and 2-10 & 30/34 Hawthorne Grove. The one which fell at the junction of Hawthorne Grove and Wheatland Lane at the junction of Alfred Lane was subsequently removed by the B.D.S. This bomb was 550lbs weight with a two sided fuse and semi-armour piercing nose. It penetrated the road surface and reached a depth of 27 feet in solid clay. There were also a number of UXBs.

Raid No. 8, 1940
Group 6 had another busy night on **September 26th,** when approximately 100 Kilo Electron Magnesium Bombs fell. The incidents were of a minor character and consisted mainly of incendiary bombs damaging 9/15 Edgmond Street; Kelvin Road and Borough Road. Good work was done in putting out fires which would have developed into major outbreaks if they had not been tackled in the early stages. There were no casualties.

Wallasey High School for Girls received a direct hit on 30 August 1940. This is a view of the west end of the Hall Balcony showing the hole in the roof caused by the bomb. Other properties in Mount Pleasant Road also received direct hits

Raid No. 9, 1940

On September 29/30th there was another raid, when H.E. large calibre bombs fell, three of which were fitted with delayed action fuses. The one at the rear of Southcroft Road exploded on impact and caused a considerable amount of damage due to the fact that it fell on a stack of concrete slabs and its penetration was thereby reduced to approximately four feet. Damage was inflicted as follows:- Buckingham Road; 7-13 Southcroft Road, with two males slightly wounded; Falkland Road; Rudgrave Square; Wright Street; Wallacre Park; Hillside Road allotments and Pauls recreation ground.

During September, Merseyside had 28 raids. Liverpool was bombed 16 times, Bootle 9, Birkenhead 11, Wallasey 9, and Crosby 4 times.

1940, OCTOBER.

October was a much quieter month, there being only 15 raids on Merseyside. Bombs fell on Liverpool 14 times, Birkenhead 7, Bootle 6 and Wallasey 3 times. These three raids caused considerable damage to property.

Raid No. 10, 1940

On October 11th, Kilo electron magnesium bombs fell with slight damage to Wheatland Lane and North Reserve including an incendiary at the Great Float Hotel which burnt itself out on a billiard table. There were no casualties.

No. 19 Grosvenor Road New Brighton showing a bomb crater

Raid No. 11, 1940

On October 14th H.E. bombs caused damage to 2-8 Bedford Road; where one male & one female were slightly injured; 42/44 & 87/89 Withens Lane; where one male & two females were slightly injured; 5/11 Linden Grove; three females slightly injured; Kirk Cottages; 3-7 Longland Road; Wallasey Golf Links; Junction Bayswater Road & Harrison Drive; St Mary's Church; Sunken Area and gun emplacements on the Promenade, where two males were killed & one seriously injured.

Raid No. 12, 1940

On October 19th H.E. bombs of a fairly heavy calibre caused damage in Belgrave Street; 26-30 & 40/42 Conningsby Drive; Merton Road; 2 Tancred Road; 16-24 Hazeldene Avenue; 3-9 Wallasey Road, including Burton's shop; rear of Coronation Buildings and on the trench shelters in Belvidere Recreation Ground. These shelters consisted of two main wings, one on each side of the entrance, and the occupants this night had crowded into one wing; the other, partly waterlogged, was entirely demolished. This was, indeed, a fortunate escape.

Total casualties for the night were one male & one female killed and one male and one female slightly injured.

1940, NOVEMBER.

During November there were fewer raids than October, but they were heavier – nine in all.

Raid No. 13, 1940

The raid on the Borough on **November 1st** took place during a very heavy thunderstorm, when many of the barrage balloons were struck by lightning. High Explosive bombs of a very heavy calibre fell on 95 Rowson Street; 13/19 Grosvenor Road; Cressingham Road; Dalmorton Road; 30/32 Tollemache Street; 31 Vyner Road; 3 Albert Street & 137/139 Victoria Road. Unfortunately, there were eight casualties of which five were fatal. The raid was confined to the New Brighton area where the Wardens did some fine work. The surprise visit of the King and Queen on

November 5th 1940 to the bombed areas of Wallasey, thrilled all those who were able to join in welcoming their Majesties.

There was a minimum of formality and cheering crowds welcomed them as they walked freely along the streets – a genuine warm-hearted, spontaneous welcome of a free people, anxious to show their undivided loyalty and affection for a King and Queen who have always displayed a ready and understanding sympathy for those who have suffered.

Their Majesties showed evident anxiety for the welfare of the many sufferers and with their gracious Royal sympathy chatted with war time workers, encouraged them and wished them luck. They visited the damaged houses of the workers and chatted with the Wardens about their duties and expressed admiration to the Chief Warden of the work the Wardens were doing. At each incident the local Wardens were on parade, and were all spoken to by their Majesties.

The Chief Warden and others in our Service had the honour of being presented to their Majesties, who received them in a delightfully informal manner.

Raid No. 14, 1940

On November 12th H.E. bombs of a very high calibre fell in the dock area including Cheshire Goods Yard and Gorsey Lane Gas Works; also 2-6 Claughton Drive; 378 Poulton Road and Mill Lane Yard. The Claughton Drive bomb, though not of a very high calibre, broke windows half a mile away. Nine people were slightly injured.

Raid No. 15, 1940

November 22nd a H.E. bomb of medium calibre, which was an odd bomb at the end of a stick, fell across Birkenhead Docks landing at the rear of the Swan Hotel Dock Road causing no casualties.

Raid No 16, 1940

November 28/29 of which there are no records.

Up to the end of November, 1940, from practically 100 raids, the total number of casualties in the Merseyside area was:—

Liverpool	669 killed.	712 seriously injured		
Bootle	44 "	82		
Birkenhead	49 "	147	"	"
Wallasey	19 "	18	"	"

1940, DECEMBER.

During the latter part of November and well into December, the enemy was not very active, but in the heavy raids of Christmas week, Wallasey suffered severely and there were many casualties, the total in the Borough being 119 killed and 91 seriously injured. Damage was very considerable.

Raid No. 17/18/19, 1940

December 20/21/22.

The bombing on the first two nights, in particular the outset of the attack, was heralded by large numbers of incendiary bombs being dropped. These were followed by parachute mines and H.E. bombs of all calibres, including armour piercing and delayed action types. The nights were rather dark and flares were used extensively by enemy aircraft.

Starting early in the evening, about 6 p.m., on **December 20th,** the first raid lasted nearly 10 hours, until 4 a.m. the following morning. On the **21st** a much heavier enemy force made their appearance about the same time, and the raid then lasted until 5 a.m. This was the longest night of the year and the Luftwaffe made good use of it. During these raids the enemy came over in waves which reached a peak from 7 to 10 p.m., and from midnight until about 4 a.m., when it seemed as though the stream of arriving aircraft would never end.

Damage to shop Nos. 53-61 Brighton Street 20 December '40

Bombs were falling continuously, and a fire situation arose which overtaxed the resources of the local Services. On the night of **December 21st,** which seemed interminable, the raid was more intense than the previous night, and Wallasey suffered seriously. The problem of housing and feeding the homeless was a heavy one, but the Services concerned tackled it heroically. Workers strove to quell the fires and release the trapped victims. Eventually, towards daybreak, our own guns ceased firing, or continued to fire desultorily.

Truly, the two nights were terrifying ones, although the bursting shells, tracer bullets shot through the sky in lines of red and orange, and the dropping pendant flares, were sights never to be forgotten.

On the third night, **December 22nd,** the enemy were heard overhead, and sirens began to wail again at almost the same time; the fires still burning made an easy target, but only a few bombs were dropped. It was Manchester that had to bear the brunt of the attack, and Merseyside breathed more freely. Of Wallasey's 119 victims during the three nights, 13 were elderly inmates of a widows' home.

The Rescue and First Aid Services worked with great courage, and saved many lives. The Fire Brigade had a heavy task. The W.V.S. gave food and comfort to the homeless, and the Wardens, as always the backbone of Civil Defence, carried out their numerous duties, helped in the fire-fighting, rescue work, and first aid, and gave that necessary confidence to the people which stiffened the morale of the whole population.

The casualties during these three days were:-
121 fatally injured, 102 seriously injured and 156 slightly injured.

Damage was caused right across the Borough including the following:-

Pickering Road
Dovedale Road.
Hamilton Road
Longdale Road
Mount Road
Wellington Road
Cavendish Road
Aylesbury Road
Bowden Road
Cambridge Road
Dalmorton Road
Vaughan Road
108,231,249 Seabank Road
Kinnaird Road
Turret Road
Castle Road
Mount Pleasant Rd
Malpas Road
6 Melling Road
Gordon Road
Harvey Road
Holland Road
Penkett Road
Earlston Road
Sandrock Road
Mornington Road
102 Urmson Road
Manor Road (Corner)
Trafalgar Road
Liscard Road
Rivington Road
Lumley Road
Gorsebank Road
218/220 Poulton Road
Kingsley Road
Ladyewood Road
Wallasey Road
Kenilworth Road
Palatine Road.
Florence Road
Eastcroft Road
Rufford Road
Station Road
Palmerston Road
Wallacre Road
Knaresborough Road
Braemore Road
Uppingham Road
Radstock Road
Probyn Road
Sandiways Road
Chapelhill Road
Bermuda Road
Durban Road
Hoylake Road
Albion Street
Rowson Street
(SS Peter & Paul Fire)
Belgrave Street
Demesne Street
Cranford Street
Vale Drive
St. Winifreds Road
Strathcona Road
Dalton Road
Serpentine Road
Bell Road
Withington Road
Walsingham Road
Barrington Road
Clifford Road
Leominster Road
Hampstead Road.
Broughton Road
Kelvin Road
Birkenhead Road
Hillcroft Road
Dawlish Road
Monmouth Road
Lymington Road
Hillside Road
Millthwaite Road
Merton Road
Claremount Road
Russell Road
Leyburn Road
Pasture Road
Camsdale Road
Leasowe Road
Zig-Zag Road
Netherton Road
Duke Street
Hope Street
Clwyd. Street
Brighton Street
Beatrice Street
Mostyn Street
Harrison Drive

Three ladies were killed at No.61 Withens Lane, which is seen here reduced to rubble on the corner of Urmson Road. The house pictured next door at No. 63 has also suffered damage. Note the white markings on the kerb stones and also on the wall which were an aid to people travelling at night when no street lighting was allowed

Molyneaux Drive
Grosvenor Drive
Radnor Drive
Magazine Lane
61 Withens Lane (Old Ladies Home)
Manor Lane
Wheatland Lane
Gorsey Lane & Gas Works
School Lane
Ditton Lane
Clare Crescent
Blenheim Road (The Andrew Gibson Home)
Imperial Avenue
Rockpoint Avenue
Chatsworth Avenue
Chepstow Avenue (Corner)
Courtenay Avenue
Croxteth Avenue
Francis Avenue
Heathbank Avenue
Moreton Market Gardens
Vicarage Grove
Wallasey Village
Spring Vale
Promenade Wall (Nr. Manor Road)
Promenade Wall (Harrison Drive)
Liscard & Poulton Railway Station
St Hilarys Church Yard
Vernons Playing Fields
Railway Embankment (Wallasey Village Stn.)

Woodlands Drive
Denton Drive
Elgin Drive
Rake Lane
Greenwood Lane
Mill Lane
Windsors Garage
Hay Lane
Bellfield Crescent
Fairfield Crescent
Brockley Avenue
Broadway Avenue
Ilford Avenue
Folly Gut
Silverlea Avenue
Haig Avenue
Joan Avenue
Kingsway
Fieldway
Agnes Grove
Saughall Massie
Coronation Buildings
Central Park
St Albans School

WARDENS – GROUP BY GROUP IN DECEMBER, 1940 [see page 27 for Group areas]

GROUP 1.

H. E. bombs fell in Albion Street; Bellfield Crescent; Duke Street; Dovedale Road; Hamilton and Langdale Roads; Molyneux Drive; Mount Road; Rowson Street; Wellington and Cavendish Roads and Brockley Avenue. There were many casualties, some fatal; burst mains and many hundreds of incendiary bombs causing fires which were tackled by the Wardens as though that had been their only previous occupation. The first aid work, as usual in this Group, was very good and several trapped people were rescued, the work going on at times

Group 1 – damage caused to Nos 5 & 7 Langdale Road

Group 2 – Nos 69-75 Dalmorton Road where the roof has been blown off. Note the barage balloon in the background

when wreckage was well alight. Several Wardens lost their homes and many suffered casualties and shock, but they carried on without fear for their own safety, and long after the "all-clear" had sounded they were busy evacuating people to safety and shelter.

GROUP 2.

The area of Post 2A had a particularly busy time and the other parts in a lesser degree. Here, as in Group I, many Wardens lost their homes and some were injured. There were many fatal casualties and damaged gas and water mains. The Wardens did excellent work looking after the homeless, rescuing trapped people, and extinguishing innumerable fires caused by incendiaries which fell on roads, gardens, houses, shops and open spaces. H.E. bombs fell in the following roads, doing considerable damage to property – Aylesbury, Bowden, Cambridge, Dalmorton, Vaughan and Seabank Roads; Clwyd Street; Magazine Lane; Kinnaird, Turret, Castle, Mount Pleasant, Melling, Gordon and Harvey Roads; Rake Lane; Woodlands Drive; Malpas Road; Grosvenor Drive and Rock Point Avenue.

GROUP 3.

Although there were a considerable number of incidents and numerous fires in the area of the Group, casualties were few. H.E. bombs fell in Holland Road; Denton Drive; Penkett Road; Manor Lane; Seabank, Earlston, Sandrock, Mornington, St. Winifred's and Urmson Roads; Withens Lane; Broadway Avenue; Kingsway, Fieldway, Radnor and Elgin Drives, Strathcona, and Dalton Roads. The incident in Sandrock Road caused considerable damage and many people were rendered homeless. After the raids the Head Warden reported that his Wardens had performed their duties under very trying circumstances with the most commendable zeal, courage and discipline, to the point of exhaustion.

GROUP 4.

*Shortly after the alert on Friday, **December 20th** 1940, showers of incendiaries fell in the area from Central Park to the shore. Most of the fires were quickly put out by Wardens with the help of the public. Meanwhile, H.E. bombs were being dropped mainly round the shore area, directed at the shipping in the river, causing a great deal of blasting round the*

Promenade area. H.E. bombs hit the Promenade Wall; the corner of Manor Road; Belgrave Street; Chatsworth Avenue; Trafalgar Road; Serpentine Road; and Chepstow Avenue corner was hit by a parachute mine. These bombs caused several casualties and a considerable number of people had to be rescued from debris and dangerous buildings. There was great damage to property and the timely evacuation of residents in the vicinity of bombs that went off some time later probably saved many casualties. H.E. bombs also fell in Vicarage Grove; Greenwood Lane; Agnes Grove; Liscard Road; Central Park and the grounds of the Andrew Gibson Homes. There were some grievous incidents, one at Withens Lane causing three fatal casualties and another at the Roger Fletcher Home. This home had always received special care from the Wardens on account of the old ladies living there, but this night it received a direct hit which resulted in 13 fatal casualties, due to being trapped under debris and gassed by broken mains. The work in this Group was remarkably good. Wardens, N.F.S., First Aid parties, working throughout the long night and days and caring little when the bombing was at its height.

GROUP 5.

The Wardens in this Group were kept very busy. Dozens of fires occurred, some attended to by the N.F.S., but mostly they were extinguished in their early stages by the Wardens with the help of civilians. Damage to property was heavy and there was much loss of life. Many fine rescue feats were effected in which the Wardens assisted the fine teams of the Rescue Parties. It was in this Group that the Service suffered it first fatal casualty when Senior Warden L.W. Goodson died from injuries received while doing his duty during the raid on **December 22nd 1940.** H.E. bombs fell in Bell Road; Liscard, Rivington, Withington, Lumley, Walsingham and Birnam Roads; the tennis courts and bandstand in Central Park; Silverbeech, Mollington, Gorsebank, Barrington, Poulton, Clifford, Kingsley, Leominster, Ladyewood, Hampstead, Wallasey and Broughton Roads.

Group 5 – Nos 48-52 Leominster Road

GROUP 6.

There were not many incidents in this Group but, owing to the small number of Wardens, they had to work at considerable pressure, and they did their job with the greatest efficiency. The fires were quickly got under control and property saved. Water mains were damaged and gas mains caught fire. Roads were blocked and H.E. bombs did much damage in the following roads:- Kenilworth; Brougham; Palatine; Kelvin; Florence; Brighton Street; Wheatland Lane; Demesne Street; Beatrice Street and Birkenhead Road. There were several fatal casualties and Wardens gave great help to the Rescue Parties relieving persons trapped in debris.

GROUP 7.

The area of this Group was covered with a vast number of incendiary bombs causing many fires and much damage. The Wardens worked like heroes and each and every one deserved special mention. Gas and water mains were fractured, the gas mains catching fire. There were many trapped people and casualties, and the Wardens worked through nights and days with the Rescue Parties and the First Aid Squads. The fire at the

Below: Group 4 – 1 to 7 Chatsworth Avenue

gas works was a serious one - and incendiary bombs fell directly on the gas container in the Gorsey Lane yard, and the fire burnt for a long while. H.E. bombs fell on houses in the following roads, causing fatal casualties and doing considerable damage:- Eastcroft, Hillcroft, Poulton, Rufford and Dawlish Roads; Cranford and Mostyn Streets; Heath Bank; Station Road; Liscard and Poulton Station; Ilford Avenue; Monmouth, Palmerston and Lymington Roads; Courtenay Avenue; Gorsey Lane and Vernons' playing fields.

Above: Group 11 – Digg Lane Moreton

GROUP 8.

A considerable number of H.E. bombs and incendiaries fell in the area of the Group: in St Hilary's Church Yard; Folly Gut; Silverlea Avenue; Mill Lane; School Lane; Clare Crescent; Wallacre and Hillside Roads; Croxteth Avenue; Knaresboro', Millthwaite, Braemore and Merton Roads; St Alban's Schools; Uppingham and Claremount Roads. Heavy damage was caused to property from blasts over a wide area and roads were impassable - but the Group was fortunate in being free from casualties. Trapped people were quickly released and many small fires were extinguished before serious damage could be done, but heavy damage was caused to the shops in Coronation Buildings. It was here that the Wardens had the privilege of assisting the A.F.S. from Bebington The Victoria Central Hospital had to be completely evacuated owing to damage caused by

Below: Group 8 – Two men are viewing the damage to property at Nos 2-10 Croxteth Avenue

bombs falling on adjacent property after 86 casualties had been received from the raids on **December 20th and 21st 1940.** The boiler house and steam boilers were completely out of action and roofs and windows of the wards were extensively damaged. The hospital was reopened on **January 13th, 1941.**

GROUP 9.

The first bombs to fall in this area on **December 21st 1940** were on the Promenade at Harrison Drive. Shortly afterwards they fell in Radstock; Russell and Probyn Roads and on the railway embankment at Wallasey Village station. This was the first real test that the Group had experienced, and the work of rescue and attending to old people was most creditable.

There were many fires and large patches of grass and gorse on the golf links had to be dealt with. On the following night bombs fell in Leyburn Road where there were fatal casualties and people trapped; Harrison Drive and Spring Vale, where there were more casualties; Windsor's Garage; Sandiway and Wallasey Village. Much property was saved from fire by the timely efforts and help of the Home Guard. From 6.25 p.m. for 12 hours, through the long night the work went on and when the "raiders passed" sounded there were many homeless people to look after. Lives were not only saved, but the good humour courage, and cheerfulness of the Wardens were said to have helped to save the reason of those rescued.

GROUPS 10 & 11.

The Wardens in the Leasowe and Moreton areas had a most trying time owing to the scattered nature of their area. Thirty-five H.E. bombs fell in the area in the Christmas week, in the following places- Pasture and Chapelhill Roads; Hay Lane; Carnsdale Road; Saughall Massie; Bermuda Road; Haig Avenue; Hoylake Road: the Market Gardens; Fairfield Crescent; Francis Avenue; Joan Avenue;

Left: Houses in Warren Drive – after raids on 12/14 March 1941

1941, JANUARY and FEBRUARY

Compared with December, these months were comparatively quiet.

Raid No. 20, 1941

January 3rd

A bomb dropped on the Navy League Grounds, Withens Lane, with fortunately no casualties. This was an isolated, incident and according to the Military Authorities this bomb was of the heaviest calibre carried by German Aircraft, The crater was about 60 ft across and the bomb penetrated to the rock strata about 18 ft below the surface.

Raid No. 21, 1941 January 9th

In Group 1 there were incidents at Sandringham Drive, Albion Street and Atherton Street resulting in two deaths and serious casualties with considerable damage to property. Rescue workers and First Aid Parties were quickly on the scene, and help was given to the Wardens by the Military. The work of the Wardens was highly commendable, especially at "Edenhurst" Albion Street, where they were immediately on the scene and rescued two young children and gave timely attention to their injuries. 63 Albion Street also received damage.

In Group 8 on the same night, considerable damage was caused at 187 Wallasey Road and Pennine Road. At this incident patrols from the Home Guard (D Coy.) gave valuable help. Bombs also fell in Creekside (near the docks); 2 Sandringham Drive; Warrens Yard and Dock Road. The bombs dropped, were of fairly heavy calibre except in the case of one at the rear of 187 Wallasey Road which was of the heaviest calibre and penetrated to the rock strata and formed a crater about 70 ft across. On the Leasowe Embankment two bombs fell side by side, one exploded and the other failed. The casualties were two Fatally injured, one Seriously injured and eight Slightly injured.

Dutton Lane, Digg Lane; and Netherton Road. Considerable damage was done to houses, farm buildings, and gas and water mains, and there was much loss of life, particularly in Chapelhill Road where two bombs fell, and in Carnsdale Road where one fell. Eight people were killed and a considerable number sent to hospital; 36 were treated at the First Aid Post and 130 at the Rest Centre; 42 homes were rendered uninhabitable. Several Wardens were injured and much difficulty was experienced in locating UXB's in the open country, but there was no relaxing until they had all been found. The Moreton Superintendent and the Head Wardens spoke in glowing terms of the work of the Wardens in attending to the trapped and injured and in extinguishing fires and finding shelter and food for bombed out people, and in co-operation with the Police, and Rescue Service and Fire Service. During these raids in December, 1940, more than 50 Wardens lost their homes, and many received serious injuries, whilst many more with minor wounds and shock carried on with their duties, notwithstanding their inconvenience.

Above: Windsor's Garage, Wallasey Village and
Left: All that remains of "Darley Dene", a house in Breck Road, after being hit by a bomb in March 1941

19

Above: *City Caterers' Cafe building in Harrison Drive*
Right: *Looking across to Foxhey Road from Breck Road after a raid in March 1941*

Raid No. 22/23/24 1941
March 12th, 13th and 14th

The second period of sustained attack, which covered a period of three nights, came in March, 1941. It was marked by the dropping on the Borough of a number of parachute mines, which were widely distributed, most Groups having one or more, in addition to the usual complement of incendiaries and high explosive. Again the Civil Defence Services did their jobs well, although without previous practical experience of the effect of parachute mines.

March was the worst month for Wallasey. Whether by accident or design, Cheshire bore the brunt of the attack, for Birkenhead also suffered very severely. On these three nights came the most brutal bombing attack of the war. The Service had been well tested by this time, and the Wardens went about their work in a masterly manner, and the people endured the suffering with fortitude. Owing to the enormous number of bombs that were dropped all over the Borough and the widespread damage from blast and fires, it is impossible to enumerate all the incidents.

The co-operation of all the Services was most marked; the Messengers, though young in years did the work of grown men without thought of danger and with amazing cheerfulness. The Fire Service was again splendid, although, in many instances, hampered through lack of water. The fire watchers and the public were of great assistance and prevented many fires from taking a hold.

The heaviest part of the attack was in the area covered by Claremount Road & district and Wallasey Village stretching down to the docks; probably due to the decoy fires being lit on the West Cheshire Golf Links, Bidston Moss.

Casualties were heavy but, taking into consideration the intensity of the raids, and the amount of damage to property, it was fortunate that the toll was not a great deal heavier.

The Rescue and Demolition Parties did very valuable work and did not spare themselves to recover the living and the dead at top speed, often carrying on at great personal risk from fires which raged all around. Early in the attack the water supply

Above: *Wallasey Village with Lycett Road on the left behind the helpers clearing debris from the road after March attacks*
Right: *A Shelter in the Lancaster Road area is almost buried under rubble after a bombing raid in March 1941. It was in this locality that a baby girl of a few months old was found alive having been buried for over three days. Both the child's parents were killed but having been taken to Victoria Central Hospital, the baby made a remarkable recovery*

for fire-fighting failed completely, the main supply pipes having been fractured by bombs. An emergency pipe line with pumps was laid from the docks to Liscard.

Very heavy damage was done in the area around Church Street, where numerous bombs and mines fell and caused many casualties, and trapped people. Although the First Aid Depot was badly wrecked, the injured taken in received immediate treatment in the light of oil lamps and flash lamps, in as calm and efficient a manner as if the workers were doing their job in normal times, and the highest praise is due to them.

Post 3A was hit and badly damaged but there were no serious injuries to the Wardens.

For the second time, the Victoria Central Hospital had to be completely evacuated because of failure of gas, water and electricity supplies. Despite this and the fact that all windows were again destroyed, 50 casualties were received during the second night of raids but were removed to other hospitals the next day.

In Group 4 terrible havoc was caused in the centre of the Borough when Lancaster Avenue and Wimbledon Street were hit. Here there were 30 fatal casualties, many of them occurring in a communal shelter, and one of the strangest episodes of all blitzed Britain took place when a Rescue Party, working in Lancaster Avenue heard the faint cry of a child. With the greatest care they worked their way to where a baby a few months old was lying buried. The child had lain there three and a half days, from the time the bomb exploded in the early morning of the fateful **March 12th 1941,** to the time of rescue on the Sunday morning – a really remarkable rescue, almost incredible, but true. The child's father and mother were both killed in the blitz, in fact their bodies protected the child from harm. The baby was taken to the Victoria Central Hospital and responded to treatment.

New Brighton Cricket Clubhouse, stand and ground are seen in Rake Lane following a bombing raid on 2/3 May 1941

In Group 8 H.E. bombs fell in all parts. Post 8C had a narrow escape when a small calibre bomb fell within 5 yards, and the only damage to the post was that it was shifted badly off its damp course. The incident in School Lane was pathetic inasmuch that damage and injury chiefly affected the old age pensioners' bungalows and their occupants. Serious fires occurred at the Water Tower in Mill Lane and at Hebron Hall. Shops in Liscard Village had a narrow escape from a direct hit.

A tragic incident occurred in Erskine Road which was almost completely demolished. A serious fire also occurred and there were a number of fatal casualties, one of which was Warden J. Jefferson, who lost his life helping in the rescue work. Another Warden, W. C. Rae, also lost his life while on duty in Clifford Road. Both these Wardens were in Group 5. In the area round Wallasey Village and St Hilarys Church the incidents were very numerous. The whole area was intensely sprinkled with incendiary bombs, many of the explosive type, causing numerous fires which were quickly tackled with stirrup pumps and in no case from these did any serious fire occur. Close on the heel of the incendiaries came the H.E.s, causing considerable damage and loss of life. In Group 9 on the night of **March 13/14th 1941,** the Wardens suffered heavily. Wardens P. Armstrong, W. W. Grisdale, Miss K. Sheridan, H. Thorpe and F. Whitehouse all lost their lives while gallantly carrying out their duties. The Head Warden received serious injuries as also did his Deputy, and many other Wardens from the mine which exploded close to Post 9B. The Coliseum Picturedrome was destroyed by fire and on the water supply failing the fires caused by H.E. among the debris assumed gigantic proportions, and the Wardens, working through long hours with total disregard for their own safety, performed many acts of bravery.

Group 7 had a very strenuous two nights when there were incidents in every sector of the

The Union Jack flies defiantly above the damage caused by the bombing to property in Eleanor Road, Moreton, on the night of 7/8 April 1941

Group. In all, there were 141 H.E. bombs, 8 para-mines, and countless incendiary bombs dropped. In one case nine fatal casualties were recorded as well as 13 others seriously injured. St. Luke's Church was hit by incendiary bombs and the roof badly burned. Extensive damage was done to shops and houses in all parts of the Group area. For his high courage and devotion to duty Messenger Low, attached to this Group, was officially commended. The Wardens worked all through the nights and days helping in many ways, while the fire watchers gave assistance in helping to put out fires; 28 Wardens lost their homes or had them severely damaged.

From the effect of these raids a large part of the Borough was rendered uninhabitable; 11 churches were hit, the electricity works and both the gas holders in Seacombe were rendered useless, and the pumping station in Seaview Road received heavy damage. The Borough certainly seemed in a bad way, sadly knocked about, and with its services out of action it looked for a while like total evacuation, but the work of reinstatement was manfully put in hand, temporary services were set up, and with the outside areas coming to our aid we were able to lick our wounds and carry on, though our eyes were heavy from want of sleep, yet with head erect and spirit undaunted.

These three nights passed and again there was a pause in the attack, and the work of restoration was put in hand. Over 10,000 people in all were rendered homeless and had to be helped temporarily in Rest Centres, and provided with temporary accommodation or new homes. During this month (March, 1941) there were 186 people killed, 196 seriously injured and 251 slightly injured in the Borough, and the Civil Defence Services received their greatest test, enduring in full measure the blood, toil and sweat that the Prime Minister said would be our lot, but with skill, courage and endurance they kept themselves alive and working, winning through to a glorious victory.

Raid No. 25, 1941
April 8th.
H.E. bombs of a fairly high calibre were dropped in the Moreton area, causing damage to several houses in Borrowdale Road; Joan Avenue; Eleanor Road; Serpentine Road; Harwarden Avenue; Karslake Road and Hawthorne Road. Fortunately, there were no casualties, and the prompt removal of people from the houses close to delayed action bombs, no doubt helped in this direction.

Winston Churchill making a suprise visit to Wallasey 25 April 1941. Sandbags can be seen in the background in Dock Road, Wallasey, the Swan Hotel is on the right

An Unexploded parachute mine which fell in a field near Bermuda Road, Moreton, on 27 April 1941

April 25th 1941

Winston Churchill made a visit to Wallasey during his surprise tour of Merseyside. He toured in an open car wearing his nautical cap and reefer coat; gas mask slung over his shoulder and cigar In mouth.

Raid No. 26, 1941

April 27th.

In the early hours of Sunday two para-mines were dropped in the fields near to Bermuda Road. Only one exploded which only made a crater in the field and broke windows of surrounding property (see photograph above).

1941, MAY. For nearly two months the people of Merseyside waited the next onslaught, which turned out to be the most desperate attempt to destroy the Port of Liverpool, the dock area being the primary target on eight successive nights. Fortunately for Wallasey, the enemy's standard of bombing was more accurate than previously, and the number of incidents in the Borough was relatively few. It was, however, a test of the endurance of Civil Defence, for Wardens had their jobs to do by day and then be out on their beats for many hours night after night. Most of them took the opportunity of getting much-needed sleep between their return from work and the sounding of the sirens, which came with monotonous regularity about the same time each evening during the eight days.

It remains to add that never was the Warden Service so large in number that duty rotas could be organised to operate during air raids. All available were expected to be on duty whenever the siren sounded during the night, and to their credit they did not fail.

Raid No. 24, 1941

Liverpool, Bootle and Birkenhead took the main weight of the attack, which started at 10.50pm on the night of **May 1st 1941,** when the first bomb, H.E, of medium calibre,

fell in Wallasey. Considerable damage was done to the docks, warehouses and shipping, and huge fires raged for days. Public utility services suffered severe damage and thousands of people were rendered homeless. On the King's Parade one of the bombs was a delayed action type, exploding some hours later. In Upton Park little damage was done. There were also bombs dropped in the docks with damage to warehouses and shipping. Improved arrangements were quickly put in hand, mobile canteens and field kitchens were provided so that no one went hungry. After eight nights of continuous bombardment from the air, the enemy exhausted himself, but it was some days before the life of the great port was anything like normal. The work of the Military and the organised labour groups drafted to the area did wonderful work in restoring the services and cleaning up the debris.

During May, the casualties were as follows:—

	Killed.	Seriously Injured.
Liverpool ...	1,435	1,065
Bootle	262	26
Birkenhead ...	28	44
Wallasey	3	19

Raid No. 28, 1941

Mav 2/3rd a parachute mine was dropped on New Brighton Cricket ground in Rake Lane, many of the properties in the locality were damaged by the blast. In total eleven people were slightly injured. A stick of medium calibre bombs fell on the foreshore at Harrison Drive; no damage was caused.

Raid No. 29, 1941

May 3/4th in Wallasey, H.E. medium calibre bombs fell on Belvidere, Cliff, Kent, Breck, Burnside, Princess (1st Aid Post), Wallasey, Leander, Laburnum (tennis courts) and Stourcliffe Roads: Hazeldene: Oakdale and Courtenay Avenues; Mostyn and Parry Street; also Rake Lane and Cemetery.

Damage in Grosvenor Road
following a raid on 7/8 May 1941

1941, June.
Raid No. 33, 1941

On June 1st Group 1 had several incidents when eight H.E. bombs fell in the St. George's Park area and Grosvenor Drive. Despite extensive damage to property, casualties were light, but Wardens suffered injuries and Warden W. J. Smythe lost his life, being instantly killed when a bomb fell in the park. We know that Wardens must be exposed to personal danger but it was doubly unfortunate that our loss should have been so heavy when the raid was not severe. His death caused the deepest regret. The fire at Apperley's Garage in Rowson Street, where the petrol pumps caught fire, was put out before then arrival of the N.F.S. The work of the Wardens especially at Post 1B was particularly good. Bombs also fell in Hardy Avenue and Bermuda Road, Moreton; and in Stringhey Road; Duke Street; St Georges Mount and St James Road. During this raid a strange missile dropped in Ailsa Road which puzzled the Wardens for a while. It looked like a C.I. downspout, 5 ft. long, but turned out to be a reminder that the men of the Royal Artillery, manning the Rocket guns, were doing their bit.

Raid No. 34, 1941

On **June 25th** H.E. bombs of a medium and heavy calibre fell in the following areas – Vaughan Road; Dalmorton Road; Seabank Road; Gorsedale Road; Westbank Avenue; Magazine Lane; Dock, Kelvin, Dalton and Oakdale (bowling Green) Roads; which caused much damage but only one person was seriously and one slightly injured.

October 20th. Bombs in Irish Sea (Harrison Drive).

October 22nd. Bombs in River Mersey.

Raid No. 35, 1941

On the night of **November 1st** Group 9 had a busy time when H.E. bombs of fairly large calibre fell in Prospect Vale; Beverley Road; Vyner Road; Studley Road; Sandy Lane and Broadway Avenue (Benyon's Nurseries). Rain started to fall at 10 o'clock on this Saturday night, and the Wardens did splendid work in rescuing people trapped and attending to the injured under very trying conditions. There were two fatal casualties.

The really good organisation of the Borough Services was again illustrated here, for although there was a breakdown in the gas, water and electricity services in a limited area, the following morning all three services were again functioning.

January 10th 1942
The last bomb fell in the Merseyside area.

Raid No. 30, 1941

On the **4/5th May** the majority of bombs dropped were of H.E. high calibre with the one in Burnside Avenue being a parachute mine. They caused damage in Roseberry Avenue; 15 Grosvenor Road; Burnside Avenue; Fender Lane; Burdens Field; 10 Tiverton Avenue; Wallasey Grammar School Grounds; The Mount, Manor Lane and Wellington Road. The casualties were three Fatal, five serious and eight slightly.

On the **6th May** a considerable number fell in the open country in Moreton, and in Mill Lane; Vale Park; Holland, Hartington and Ashburton Roads.

Raid No. 31, 1941

On the **7/8th May** all the bombs dropped were of a light, medium and heavy calibre causing damage in Rolleston Drive; Lyndhurst Road; Victoria Road; Rowson Street; the Promenade (New Brighton); Kings Parade; Tollemache Street; Grosvenor Road; rear of Waterloo Road; Little Hope Street; 5 Windsor Street and on the ferry steamer Royal Daffodil which sank at her moorings at the Seacombe Landing Stage. Three fatal casualties occurred in the Mostyn Street incident.

Raid No. 32, 1941

On **May 31st,** a number of medium calibre H.E., bombs fell in Bowden, Halton, Shelton, and Seaview Roads; Queensway, Sudworth (rear), Gorsehill (reservoir) and Studley Roads; Big Yard Wallasey Village and in Inglewood, Cobham and Borrowdale Roads, Moreton - there were no casualties.

What then are our recollections of 1938-44? Are they the sight of streets a mass of rubble, of houses ripped open, the glare of fires, the explosions, noise and devastating blast, the dust and dirt and indescribable smell, the timid reply from the stairs saying "All's well"?

Are they the pain in the head and the constant pulling yourself together, and the inner call to "carry on," or the crouching beside low walls, the lying flat on the pavement and the clawing at the gutter, the everlasting tea-drinking and cigarette smoking, putting out fires, helping in the rescue, the near-misses, hidden craters in the dark, the tangled firemen's hose, trailing telephone wires, drenching rain, the cold grey dawn, the scenes of desolation and ghastly mess? Are they the want of sleep, the emotions and recollections of the night's work and its incidents generally, and the dirty worn-out appearance of our colleagues?

All these are hazy recollections, but there is nothing hazy about the fact that we found many new friends, and that, out of all the horror, Christianity instinctively came to light again for on every hand we saw that, wherever people were bombed out, they were taken in and given shelter, the hungry were fed and the people without clothing were clothed and given rest, and with this thought in mind we can look forward to the future with the utmost hope and confidence.

As a final word to this record, it might be said that although the natural characteristic of the British is for understatement and hesitation to take credit when it is due, it is thought that there will be no criticism on this account of the attempt that has been made to indicate what the Wallasey Warden Service achieved during 1938-44.

The Service was known for some time as the Cinderella of the great Civil Defence Organisation, but the Government, in their wisdom, did select a suitable name for the men and women of that Service - WARDEN - and in that capacity the pages of history will undoubtedly register that these men and women, the front line troops of Civil Defence, without any tradition or background, did a great work in sustaining the spirit and morale of our people.

Wallasey, during the first five years of war, established a record of achievement, for which it may be justly proud. Our town has a great future, and when that future has been reached, let us be in a position to say that we, for our part, maintained the Warden Spirit, and did our best, small though the contribution was to the vast whole, towards ensuring that this country of ours shall remain possessed in the years to come of all the dignity and greatness she found again in the tribulations of war.

Appointments of Chief Wardens and Deputies.

The first Chief Warden appointed was Mr. David Forsyth, who prepared and laid down carefully thought out plans for war-time mobilisation of the Warden Service. It was with great regret that in July, 1939, we learned that owing to ill health he had been compelled to relinquish his office. His departure left a blank in the organisation hard to fill for his energetic work and perseverance and organising ability laid the foundation-stone of our Service. It was necessary in the early stages to see that the organisation was built up on a progressive and resourceful basis and the high standard and efficiency that it reached reflected the energy displayed by its leader and his work called for a record of appreciation and gratitude. Mr. Forsyth was presented with an illuminated address signed by all the Head Wardens testifying to the invaluable services he rendered to our organisation.

Consequent upon Mr. Forsyth's resignation, Mr. F. D. Larcombe was appointed Chief Warden, but he only held the position for six months, when he found that he was unable to carry on owing to the strain of his duties, and he resigned in January, 1940.

The A.R.P. Controller then called upon Mr. J. Reginald Smith to act as Chief Warden. Mr. Smith was one of the first to enrol in the Service in 1937. His appointment gave general satisfaction to the Wardens by whom he was always held in the highest esteem. He came to the Warden Organisation with a good record of service during the last war, when he was with the Artists' Rifles and the Lancashire Fusiliers, acting as Gas Officer of the latter.

As Deputy Mr. George Proudman was appointed, and together they built up the organisation to its fine state of preparedness which carried it through the trying years of the war.

HEADQUARTERS' STAFF.

From the beginning of the war, day and night, the Chief Warden's Office was open for information and enquiries, and all Wardens will join in thanking the staff for their unfailing courtesy, viz.:—

Mrs. D. Stephenson.	Mr. J. H. Walker.	Mrs. E. L. Jones.
Mrs. K. M. Pennington.	Mr. W. Batterham.	Capt. W. P. Meldrum.

The following Wardens also assisted from time to time and their work was invaluable:

Mrs. K. Smith.	Mr. H. Pennington.	Mrs. G. M. Elkes.
Miss P. Johns.	Mr. V. Penn.	Mr. C. Heaton.
Mrs I Waterworth.	Mr. H.S. Kewley.	Mr. J. G. S. Clayton.

HEAD AND DEPUTY HEAD WARDENS

Group.	Head Wardens	Deputy Head Wardens.	Group.	Head Wardens.	Deputy Head Wardens.
1.	H. Kingham.	S.A. Swift.	7.	L.F. Wates.	R.W. Leyne.
	G. Proudman.			J.W.E. Albones.	E.R. MacDonald.
	E. Birchall.	W. A.Drummond.		E.R. MacDonald.	C.W. Stevens.
2.	P. Boumphrey.	H. S. West.		C.W. Stevens.	J. Montgomery.
	H. S. West.	J. Candlish.	8.	A Rowbottom.	J. Jeffries.
		A. E. Rawlinson.		J. Jeffries.	P.E. Pickstock.
3.	L. F. Turner.	E. A. Brakell.		P.E. Pickstock.	A.G. Berry.
		D. E. Bagshaw.			P.H. Sharp.
		T. G. Brandreth.	9.	F.D. Larcombe.	J.B. Smith.
4.	L. B. Edwards.	G. S. Sayle.		J.R. Smith.	H.E. Battersby.
		E. C. King.		H.E. Battersby.	P.H. Jones.
	E.C. King.	C. Wilcox.		P.H. Jones.	F.G. Brewer.
5.	W. M. Jardine.	P. J. .Wheeler.	10.	A.R. Inger.	F.G. Brewer.
	P. J. Wheeler.	R. S. Carty.			J.S. Walker.
		E. Jones.			
	E. Jones.	J. D. Booth	11.	H. Pullin.	F. Taylor
		E.Cox.			F. Ball.
6.	A. J. Francis.	H. J. Knox.			
	H. J. Knox.	J. Davies.			
		S. F. Lofthouse		Moreton Superintendent - F. Mathieson.	

INCIDENT OFFICERS

The following Wardens trained and qualified as Incident Officers

Group	Name	Qual.	Group	Name	Qual.
1.	W. A. Drummond	D.H.W.	Group 4.	G. A. L. Parfitt	S.W.
	J. McK. Dunn	S.W.			
	P. Brayfield	P.W.	Group 5.	J. Kirby	S.W.
	W. J. Thompson	P.W.		J. H. Morrell	S.W.
	T. C. Campbell			H. R. Machell	D.S.W.
	A. R. Jupp	D.S.W.		A. W. Roberts	P.W.
	F. M. Cook (Mrs.)	S.W.		A. W. Pickard	S.W.
	J. M. Cook (Miss)	D.S.W.	Group 7.	H. H. Beale	J. Jervis (Miss) S.W.
	M. A. F. Jones (Mrs.)	S.W.		C. W. Stevens	H.W.
2.	G. Askham	S.W.	Group 8.	P. E. Pickstock	H.W.
	E. Woodcock	S.W.		P. H. Smart	D.H.W.
	F. T. Saunders	D.S.W.		L. Harrison	
	J. D. Lythgoe	S.W.		W. C. Donaldson	S.W.
	C. Ross			E. W. Edwards	D.S.W.
	F. Harrison	D.S.W.		E.Hawkins	D.S.W.
	D. G. Elston (Mrs.)	D.S.W.	Group 9.	D. F. Keir	
3	A. A. McDonald	S.W.		K. Pryke	
	D. Duprey	S.W.			
	E. E. Cottrell	S.W.	Group 10.	J.S.Walker	D.H.W.
	L. F. Turner	H.W.			
	G. D. Jones (Miss)	S.W.	Group 11.	F. Ball	D.H.W.
	R. N. Morris (Miss)	S.W.		F. Mathieson	Supt.
	F. M. Gutteridge (Miss)	D.S.W.			
	K. Parry (Miss)	D.S.W.	Hd. Qtrs.	W. T. Batterham	S.W.
	V. M. Davies (Miss)	D.S.W.		E. L. Jones (Mrs.)	

BOMB RECONNAISSANCE OFFICERS

The following Wardens trained and qualified for the responsible and dangerous duty of bomb reconnaissance and special thanks are due to them for volunteering for this work:-

J. H. Walker	S.W.	Headquarters.	F. Mathieson	Supt.	Group 11.
B. Foster		Group 2.	F. Taylor	D.H.W.	Group 11.
J. Kirby		Group 5.	F. Ball	D.H.W.	Group 11.
J. A. Webster	S.W.	Group 9.			

DIVISION OF THE BOROUGH INTO GROUPS.

The Borough was divided into 11 groups, each in charge of a Head Warden and a deputy Head Warden, each Group contained 16 sectors in charge of Senior Wardens and their Deputies.

Group 1. Extended from the Promenade, New Brighton, Molnyeux Drive, Rowson Street, Field Road,
Shiel Road, Sudworth Road, and Mount Roads. Stoneby Drive, Rockland Road, Grove Road, and Sandcliffe Road to the foreshore. It included New Brighton Tower, Victoria Gardens, Winter Gardens, 2 cinemas, Portland Court Mansions, Boarding Houses, private hotels, and important residential districts and several churches and schools.
Posts.— King's Parade, St. George's Park, Sea Road.

Group 2. Location. Promenade between Dalmorton Road and Magazine Lane, through to Rolleston Drive and Belvidere Road between Grove Road and Kingsway and adjoins Group 1, It contains large schools and is mainly residential.
Posts.— Vaughan Road Schools, Coronation Avenue Schools and Elleray Park.

Group 3. Extends from the Promenade between Magazine Lane and Manor Lane and carries on through Belvidere Road between Kingsway and Meadway and adjoins Group 2. This Group contains the Grammar School and Oldershaw School and is mainly residential.
Posts.—Earlston Road, Manor Lane, Massey Park.

Group 4. Comprises the district from the Promenade between the Egremont Pier and Manor Lane through to Grosvenor Street. It includes the shopping district of King Street, Gaumont and Royal Picture Houses, and Andrew Gibson Homes; A.R.P. Headquarters and Police Station; and large schools.
Posts.—St. Columba's Church, Central Park, Concert Hall.

Group 5. The area extends from the Promenade between Egremont Ferry and the Town Hall and extends through to Poulton Road and Oxton Road, including the Town Hall, the Central Park area and large Schools.
Posts.—Central Park, Church Street Schools, Town Hall.

Group 6. Extends from the Promenade at the Town Hall to Seacombe Ferry and through to Oakdale Road and includes a portion of the Dock Road, and several large factories and mills. It is a densely populated area and suffered from lack of Wardens.
Posts.—Riverside Schools, Bridle Road, St. Paul's Recreation Ground,

Group 7. Dock Road, Oakdale Road, Poulton Road, Oxton Road, Woodstock Road, Marlowe, Lymington and Breck Roads, Broadway, Residential, industrial and dock area and schools.
Posts.—Gorsedale Road Schools, Gorsey Lane, Poulton Schools.

Group 8. Broadly this covers the centre of the Borough and the principal shopping centre of Liscard Village.
Posts.—Wellington Hotel, Belvidere Recreation Ground, St. Hilary's Gardens.

Group 9. Promenade, Harrison Drive, Sandcliffe Road, Grove Road, Belvidere Road, Broadway Avenue, Wallasey Village beyond Railway Bridge in Leasowe Road to Malvern Road on to the shore. Contains Golf Links. Mainly residential property.
Posts.—Mosslands Drive, Claremount Road Church, Harrison Drive.

Group 10. Extends from the Railway Bridge in Leasowe Road to the Borough boundary in Upton Road, Moreton. It is a scattered area and covers more ground than any two Groups in the Borough,
Posts.—Leasowe Road, Eastway Schools, Reeds Lane.

Group 11. Covers a large area consisting of most of Moreton and that part of Saughall Massie within the Borough. Owing to the widespread nature of Groups IO and 11 they were placed under the control of a Superintendent, and a Rally Centre was opened in August, 1940, which was furnished and fitted by the Wardens themselves.
Posts.—Victory Hall, Upton Road Schools, Saughall Recreation Ground and Moreton Rally Centre.

L.A.R.P. INSTRUCTORS.

Training Officer -   - Inspector A. W. Williams, B.E.M.

Group.
1. C. O. Green.
   W. J. Thompson.
   J. Me K. Dunn.
2. T.H.Burnett.
   R. L. Bryant.
3. H. Pennington.
   T. G. Brandreth.
   R. H. Harrison.

Group.
4. G. L. Parfitt,
   G. A. Griffin.
5. W. Roberts.
   Rev. F.C.Jackson.
6. S. J. Lofthouse.
   J. Wilson.
7. J. Montgomery.
8. Mrs. K. M. Pennington.
   The late W. P. Johnstsone.

Group.
9. Mrs. E. Cole.
   F. G. Brewer.
   E. A. Woolley.
11. F.Mathieson.
    H. Pullin.
    F. Ball.
    F. Taylor.
HQ. W. T. Batterham.
    J. H. Walker.

In order to have available Instructors for each Group a scheme was introduced in 1939 for selected Wardens to receive special instruction to pass the examination as L.A.R.P. Instructors. The above Wardens gave a considerable amount of time to their work and were a very valuable asset to the organisation and deserve special thanks.

POSTWARDENS.

The creation of a new position in the Service by the appointment of Post Wardens did much to improve the internal working of the Groups, and lightened the work of the Head Wardens.

The tried and trusted Wardens, one from each post who were selected for this important position carried out their duties which were many and varied in an admirable manner and grateful thanks are due to them for their hearty co-operation.

They are as follows:-

Group
1.	R. Hogg.	T.G.B. Fishwick.	W.J. Thompson.
	P. Brayfield.		
2.	G. Askham.	T. H. Burnett.	Capt. A. Sproule
3.	T. G. Brandreth.	R. H. Felton.	E. E. Cottrell
4.	J. P. Brown.	G. A. Griffin.	G. Parfitt.
			L. Colquitt.
5.	W. Millett	L. Gilbertson.	G. N. Parker.
6.	W. Garnet.	J. S. Davies.	D. Forrest.
7.	W. Hughes.	G. Gill.	W. Winstanley.
8.	E. Edwards.	F. Abrahams.	S. L. Owens.
	E. Laurie.		
9.	J. B. Yourston.	H. A. Rooksby.	F. Potter.
10.	W. B. McMillan.	G. Offllands.	J. A. Warren.
11.	F. Ball	G. Jones	S. Lee.

GAS CLEANSING IN PRIVATE HOUSES.

The scheme launched in the Borough by the Wardens in 1942 for the provision by householders of facilities in private houses for the cleansing of persons contaminated by liquid blister gas was well taken up by the residents. It was necessary for the scheme to be a success that it should have the whole-hearted co-operation of the people, and they responded cheerfully, for over 700 volunteered to provide cleansing facilities in their houses so that passers-by contaminated could have immediate attention and after a thorough wash-down be provided with sufficient clothing to proceed to their homes. The scheme was explained to householders by the Wardens who gave instructions on the use of anti-gas ointment and cards were exhibited in windows to direct people. Although no use was made of the facilities provided, the very best thanks are due for the good neighbourly spirit displayed.

The co-operation of the W.V.S. in this work was most helpful and much appreciated.

FIRE GUARDS.

The placing of the responsibility for the training and organisation of the Fire Guards on the Chief Warden and the Warden Service was a heavy job. The difficulties in the initial training and the selection of persons with gifts of leadership were not easily overcome. The Wardens, however, took them under their wing, trained them to know their sectors, and every inch of the premises they had to guard; the need of an adequate warning system and action plan, by means of which a fire could be spotted immediately and dealt with promptly; the need for good discipline; the use of cover when attacking a fire; need for reliefs and obtaining assistance; reconnaissance work; use of assembly points; tactics for preventing fire spreading, etc. The Street Fire Guards responded manfully, and they were ultimately a very valuable adjunct to the Warden Service.

On the severance of the Services, and the setting up of the Fire Guard Plan, there was some disappointment that after all our good work we were to be parted, as it was felt that the parting was for the good of neither Service.

As from September 12th, 1944, the authorities decided to suspend the operation of the Fire Guard Plan, and the responsibility of reporting all fires caused by enemy action was once again placed on the Warden Service.

CIVIL DEFENCE MESSENGER SERVICE.

This service was recruited at the beginning of the war and has rendered valuable service to all sections of Civil Defence.

The boys from the age of 16 were trained in their duties by the Chief Messenger, attended lectures and worked to rotas under their own group leaders.

During the long nights of the raids the Head Wardens reported on their high standard of courage and devotion to duty. Young in years they did the work of grown men without thought of danger and with amazing cheerfulness, and one of their members was officially commended.

Their routine work at the posts during the long stand-by periods was done in a conscientious manner, and their help to the Warden Service cannot be too highly praised.

BENEVOLENT FUND.

This fund was launched in 1940 when it was found that a fund of some description was wanted in the organisation to meet the urgent calls in cases of distress.

The objects of the fund are to provide immediate pecuniary assistance at the discretion of the executive officers in so far as the money in the fund will allow, for a widow or husband and/or dependents of any Warden whose death is due to the war, or any Warden seriously injured owing to the war, or to any Warden or his or her dependents in any other circumstances.

The fund has been maintained by the subscriptions of the Wardens, and townspeople generously gave donations and showed in this practical manner their appreciation of and gratitude for all that the Wardens had done.

The fund has been able to render assistance to several members of the Service and their dependents who have been grateful for the help readily given.

The Deputy Chief Warden, Mr. George Proudman, has acted as secretary and treasurer of the fund since its formation, and his colleagues as executive officers have been Councillor L. B. Edwards, Mr. H. S. West and Mr. H. Pullin, Head Wardens of Groups 4, 2 and 11 respectively.

In order to secure the safe working of the fund in the future a new governing Committee was formed on November 15th, 1944, to operate in post war years.

This committee consists of the Head Wardens or Deputy Head Wardens of all groups, the Chief Warden, Deputy Chief Warden and the Moreton Superintendent. It is to continue to operate for a period of five years.

FIRST AID.

There was no branch of the Wardens' work in which at one time showed such widely different standards of knowledge and efficiency, but as more responsibility was placed on the Service from time to time the Wardens realised that as casualties were in their hands for a considerable time, it was essential for them to be thoroughly trained, and special attention was given to the subject. Many Wardens received the diploma of the Red Cross and St. John's Societies, and a considerable number qualified for the life saving badge. Our thanks are due to the doctors and lecturers who gave so much of their time in lecturing to the various classes, thus enabling the Service to give such timely aid to the injured and assistance to the medical branch of Civil Defence.

WARDENS AND THE HOME GUARD.

On the formation of the Local Defence Volunteers in 1940, many male Wardens felt the urge to join and bear arms in the country's service. Such a corps naturally had a far stronger appeal to a man than our non-combatant Warden Service, but the desire had to be suppressed. Our job was not the carrying of arms but the equally important one of sustaining courage and morale and looking after the civil population.

The tendency of the authorities to recruit individual members of the Warden Service into the Home Guard in 1942 caused alarm, as it was considered that the Service, in the vulnerable area, should be maintained at full strength. The Wallasey Head Wardens, after much thought, adopted a recommendation at their conference that, in order to meet all national situations, the Warden Service be allowed to form its own armed company, officered by its own personnel, receive training as a body under the direction of the local Home Guard unit, and be attached thereto as a supernumerary or reserve force, to be called up if and when necessary. It was considered that under these conditions Wardens could carry out their C.D. duties and, where willing, could receive training in the use of modern firearms and so increase the efficiency and value of the Service.

The military authorities, who were very interested in the proposal, sent their representatives to give lectures on the role of the Home Guard and how the Wardens could be of use to the military in case of an invasion. The lectures were crowded and enthusiastic, and it is interesting to recall the keenness of the ex-Servicemen in handling a tommy-gun and pulling it to pieces. It was in April, 1942, that the Ministry of Home Security agreed to the scheme for the enrolment of the C.D. Personnel in the Home Guard, and owing to the necessity of finding replacements for the large number of regular troops in the anti-aircraft batteries who were required for service elsewhere, over 100 part-time male Wardens joined the local 104 (103 Cheshire Home Guard) Rocket A.A. Battery, R.A.

These Wardens undertook the additional duty of training and fitting themselves for the more active role of manning the guns while continuing with their work of Civil Defence, when not actually engaged on military duties. This further sacrifice of time and leisure cemented stronger than ever the bond that bound the Warden Service to the public generally. On the war situation improving, it was officially announced that as from September 11th, 1944, operational duties would be carried out on a voluntary basis, which indicated that the job was virtually completed. For over two years the battery performed operational duty nightly, and under its commanding officer, Major T.W. Harley, M.B.E., M.C. turned out to be a most admirably run battery, which achieved a high standard and reputation.

The Leasowe Home Guard practising on a 4.5 inch anti-aircraft gun situated in Telegraph Lane

PUBLIC SHELTERS

Soon after air raids on Merseyside became general and frequent, Wardens were confronted with a new problem for which little provision had been made in advance. It concerned the use of public shelters, not only after the sirens had sounded, but for regular dormitory occupation, and until the shelters were made the responsibility of a special Corporation official, the onus of trying to create order out of chaos fell to a large extent on the Warden organisation.

One difficulty, quickly apparent, was that Wardens could not spend a great deal of time in these public shelters during an alert period, as it was then their duty to patrol the streets, and the attempts to build up an organisation of shelter marshals, allocate bunks to specified occupiers, etc., came as an extra duty on the nights the siren did not sound, as the big public shelters were occupied nightly by large numbers of people, whether or not there was an air raid. In Group 1 there was the Borough's large stand believed to be strongest, public shelter, and therefore very popular – the basement of the Tower Building. As this had been originally constructed as the foundation for, and to carry the strain of the former observation tower- higher than that at Blackpool, before it was taken down – the belief in its strength was probably justified.

But that belief meant an influx of people far in excess of the number deemed suitable in the interests of comfort and hygiene. It was beyond the powers of the few Wardens available to prohibit or restrict entry, with the result that the shelter was occupied nightly by a number up to four times its official capacity, and the Wardens in whose sectors the shelter lay had a most difficult and wearying task, though they were always received with sympathy and encouragement when they made routine calls during air raids. Much of the credit for the improved organisation which was ultimately achieved was due to Canon W. S. Coad, now of Chester Cathedral, who was then vicar of St. James', New Brighton. He made it his business to call at the shelter nightly, whether there was an air raid in progress or not, and it was through his patient work, in great part, that the first shelter wardens were appointed, being representatives of the regular users of the shelter.

Thereafter, the organisation steadily, but slowly, improved and, though there was always anxiety in the minds of Warden that so large a number of people should be so assembled together, their fears of what might be the effects of a direct hit by a heavy bomb on the building itself, or on the main entrances, were never realised. The users of this shelter were undoubtedly more happy to be in it than the Wardens were to see them there in such large numbers.

In Group 1 there were two other public shelters, the Sandrock and the Palace, both used as dormitories but, being smaller, the problems were not so serious. Moreover, as both were within about a quarter of a mile of the Tower, and as the belief in the impregnability of the latter remained strong and unshaken, neither had the same problem of overcrowding. In both these shelters the Wardens were initially responsible for the selection and appointment of shelter

Damage is seen at the entrance to the Earlston Library shelter and Warden Post following the air raids on the 12/14 March 1941

These Public Shelters with pitched roofs [some others in Wallasey had flat roofs] in Palatine Road seem to have survived the bombing which has caused damage to other buildings in the street. As all lights at night were banned, the white paint on the shelter entrance and corners, could be recognised in the dark prior to a raid and accidents avoided

marshals, and it says much for the interest displayed that each shelter rapidly settled down to its new role, with an absence of squabbles and animosity, though it could never be said that the regular occupants of either were either happy or contented!

There was, in Group 1, another shelter not officially classed as a public shelter, but always ready to succour the distressed and, therefore, deserving of inclusion in this record. It was the strengthened basement – normally a gymnasium – of the Maris Stella Convent, where the Reverend Mother and Sisters gave help and encouragement to all who sought it – the bereaved, the bombed-out, and the passers-by. Wardens who called on their rounds to enquire whether all was well were fortified by welcome cups of tea, and could not but be impressed by the earnestness and solicitude of the good wishes which followed them as they resumed their patrols.

The foregoing briefly sketches shelter conditions in Group 1, and much the same was experienced in other parts of the Borough – especially Group 5, where the Head Warden took under his personal charge the arrangements necessary in regard to the use of the basement at the Town Hall. Here, as at the Tower, at one period hundreds of people flocked nightly in order to obtain a peaceful night's rest.

Special mention should be made of the Ilford Avenue Trench Shelter, where Mrs. Wheat and the users organised themselves in a splendid manner – improving as best they could the conditions obtaining in the covered trenches. It is worth while to record that among themselves they each subscribed one halfpenny for every raid-free night and a considerable sum was collected which was handed to the Wardens' Benevolent Fund in acknowledgment of the help they had received.

~ ~ ~ ~ ~ ~ ~ ~ ~ ~ ~

Support for Charities.

The Warden Service has at all times given considerable help to charities. The proceeds from their dances, whist drives and collections have been distributed to the Victoria Central Hospital, the Mayor's War Fund, Red Cross Prisoners of War Fund, the Fund for the Blind, Waifs and Strays, and the Red Cross Penny a Week Fund has been well supported.

In April, 1943, St. Dunstan's appealed to the Chief Warden to undertake a house to house envelope collection in the Borough on behalf of their institution. The appeal to the Wardens was readily

answered as the cause had their warmest support. The collection was so well organised by the Head Wardens that the result was a record of £857-8-1d.

The following year an appeal was again made to the Wardens to undertake the collection, but this time it was a joint appeal for St. Dunstan's and the Wallasey Fund for the Blind, when the previous year's record was passed and a sum of £948-4-0d. was collected.

Special thanks were received from Sir Ian Fraser, C.B.E., M.P., for the fine achievement and for the valuable work so generously undertaken.

When the appeal was lodged for comforts for the

Wardens of London and the Southern Area in 1944, Wallasey Wardens immediately responded and showed their practical sympathy for the comrades who were carrying on under the most trying conditions.

The result of the appeal was that a cheque for £71-19-10d. was forwarded to the National Civil Defence Welfare Fund.

WAR SAVINGS.

The Wardens' Saving Groups have done consistently good work with their weekly collections, and the special savings weeks in the Borough, the total amount collected to the end of 1944 being over £53,000.

Wallasey's Civil Defence Choir and Orchestra.

Wallasey can claim that she gave a lead to the country in that she was the first town to possess a Civil Defence Choir and Orchestra. First formed with a handful of medical personnel in "blitz" days, its spiritual home is the First Aid Post No. 2 in Princess Road, New Brighton. It has grown from strength to strength and now includes many members of the Warden Service. Performances have been given over a wide area, and a variety of charities have benefited considerably thereby.

The first attempt was a concert of selections from Gilbert & Sullivan Operas, given at the post in 1941. Originally, there was no orchestra. This came into being in January, 1942, when a small group, consisting of six violinists, two cellists, two viola players, and a pianist, began rehearsing.

A milestone in the history of this organisation was the memorable Easter Sunday Service in 1942, when excerpts from the "Messiah" were given at Egremont Presbyterian Church. This was considered to be the birth of the combined forces, and since then they have marched side by side. The performances given in local hospitals and churches have been much appreciated. Today the choir can take performances in "Hiawatha" and Haydn's "Creation" in their stride, and the orchestra is strong enough to give public performances of such works as Beethoven's Fifth Symphony.

Throughout, the driving force has been their conductor, Mr. Stainton de B. Taylor, who has had a long experience of choral and instrumental work; since the formation of the Society, its energetic secretary has been Mr. V. J. Tullit.

Every penny that the Society has earned by its efforts has been handed over to charity, and among the charities that have benefited are the Mayor of Wallasey's War Fund, the Prisoners of War Fund, the Civil Defence Benevolent and Welfare Funds, local charities and hospitals.

A special word of thanks is due to the choir for having put Wallasey on the musical map, and giving its people an opportunity of enjoying good music, and it is hoped that the Society will continue to flourish.

SOCIAL SIDE OF THE WARDEN SERVICE.

The social committees of the various Groups did very good work during the war years in organising whist drives and indoor sports, games; dances and concerts were held and jumble sales were organised, from all of which large sums of money were raised for local charities and the Wardens' Benevolent Fund.

Group 1 specialised in its own particular brand of cabaret, which provided much amusement. Although lacking in technical perfection of song and dance, its lyrics, both topical and personal, showed a pretty wit, and its male voice quartette were flawless in their interpretation of song and dance. This Group was fortunate in possessing some very accomplished pianists. Group 7 organised many first class concerts and contributed very largely to the Benevolent Fund and other charities, as also did Group 4 who held a weekly whist drive throughout the war period.

THE WALLASEY WARDENS' ASSOCIATION.

This association was formed to co-ordinate the work of the various Groups and to encourage a spirit of comradeship amongst all the Wardens of Wallasey and to arrange entertainments, and provide social, sports and educational facilities. Under the chairmanship of Mr. V. J. Tulitt, with Mr. G. A. Griffin as secretary and treasurer, and Mr. G. Parfitt as sports organiser, very good work was done. The dances arranged at the Tower Ballroom were most successful and provided funds for the purchase of equipment for indoor sports. Table tennis and darts tournaments were arranged at the posts, and kept the Wardens in close touch with each other. Billiards and bowls matches also brought the Wardens into contact with other branches of Civil Defence, and proved beneficial. Lectures and concerts were arranged, and the association has provided a valuable adjunct to the Service.

The Warden Service Tenders Thanks to:—

The Chief Constable, A.R.P. Controller, for the counsel and advice he has so often afforded us and for the loan of air raid damage photographs.

Inspector A. W. Williams, B.E.M., for making such a good job of our Training.

Mr. H. B. Holliday, the Gas and Water Engineer, and his key men, for the co-operation with our Service at all times.

Mr. H. R. B. Wood, M.A., Director of Education, for the accommodation so readily placed at our disposal in all parts of the Borough, and the help afforded by his school authorities.

Mr. W. Wilson, F.L.A., Chief Librarian, for lending reading matter to those doing long stand-by Post Duties.

Other branches of Wallasey's Civil Defence Services for their willing co-operation and assistance at all times.

The Editor of the "Wallasey News" for allowing the use of his columns for Wardens' Notes each week.

The Deputy Chief Warden, Mr. George Proudman, tor having undertaken the task of preparing this souvenir booklet, and Mr. Edward Birchall, M.A., for the assistance he has given.

Warden J. J. Mansfield for supplying group and individual photographs of Warden Personnel.

The various Church Authorities in the Borough who have so willingly assisted by providing accommodation for meetings, lectures, etc.

Those we have omitted to mention, but to whom we owe our thanks.

WALLASEY HOME GUARD

When Britain was drawn into the Second World War 1939-1945 the defence of the country was provided by the British Army with recruits from the Territorial Army. The Territorial Army grew out of the Territorial Force, a home defence organisation founded in 1908 and it was not until 1921 that it became known as the Territorial Army. The war in 1939 mobilized its members for action. The fall of France in 1940 left the country vulnerable to invasion and to help in its defence a new force was created to give static defence and guard against enemy parachute landings. The official title was Local Defence Volunteers but they were also known as "Parashooters".

The Volunteers were mostly ex officers and men from the First World War, too old for active service but keen to get involved and also boys under 17 too young for war. By July 1940 the name of the Local Defence Volunteers had been changed to the Home Guard.

This national volunteer body of men was accepted as part of the armed services of the Crown and as such were subject to military discipline, but they received no pay. They also had little equipment and no uniform. Some were issued with a helmet and a rifle, otherwise those without weapons found old swords, ancient shotguns, pikes, pitchforks, even gas pipes with welded bayonets. However by 1941 they did get a hat and a basic military uniform.

When the appeal for the Local Defence Volunteers was launched the Government was expecting about 150,000 to come forward in the first month; it was nothing like that. Such was the enthusiasm of the men at home to do their "bit" that by the end of the first month 750,000 had volunteered and weeks after that the figure was over two million. The number fluctuated of course when the young volunteers were conscripted but the force never fell below one million until they were disbanded 1 November 1944. The Home Guard had then been in existence for four and a half years, a wonderful body of men giving great moral support to the civilian population.

When the appeal for the Local Defence Volunteers went out nationwide Wallasey men were also keen to enrol and in the first week of the appeal nearly 2,500 came forward. William Duncan Taylor, who had been an officer in the First World War, as a Lieutenant in the East Yorkshire Regiment, was appointed as Group Commander,a man who would mould these volunteers into a fighting force known as "16th Cheshire (Wallasey) Battalion".He was also a merchant and a well known Wallasey Magistrate. He was assisted by Sidney Goodman, a school teacher, serving as a volunteer Adjutant who was later given a regular commission as a Captain/Quartermaster, with his deputy W.G. Pack; Major F. Samuel became Second in Command; the AdministrationOfficer was F. Waterworth with A.W. Heap as his deputy.; Capt. E. Marks was the Musketry Officer and the Armourer. The Battalion Headquarters were first in the Concert Hall, Manor Road, and then in June 1940 they were moved to the Oval, the home of Wallasey Cricket Club, for one month, when another move established theforce in the Drill Hall, Riverview Road, Seacombe. This was H.Q. for three years until March 1943 when

"Tynwald", 142 Grove Road was taken over. Many people will recall that this house was at one time "Tynwald School for Girls" and today it is currently owned and used by The Old Wallaseyans' Club. A total of 6,000 men enrolled in the 16th Cheshire Battalion and of those some 2,000 left to join the regular forces whilst others were drafted to anti-aircraft rocket sites and coastal defence. There were initially five Companies in the Battalion, reducing to three by August 1944. The group territory was the whole of Wallasey Borough and Bidston Moss area.

1. "A" Company was stationed at Leasowe Golf Club and had in command firstly, H.V.L. Collings, followed by L. Mickle M.C. and finally C.E. Balmforth M.C. This Company was noted for signalling and became the Specialist Weapons Company.

2. "B" Company, with 560 members, had Major F.A. Samuel DSO as a C.O. and tenanted Harrison Hall. On 1 June 1940 R.R. Atherton took over command (Samuel had gone into H.Q.) followed by Major T.H. Parsons and later Major J.0. Broster.

3. "C" Company, established in June 1940, had their base at the New Brighton Rugby Football Club ground in Reeds Lane, Leasowe with Capt. H. Pollitt in command. In December 1943 Capt. Thorpe assumed control until July 1944 when "C" Company partly merged with "B" leaving a half company at Reeds Lane. Moreton residents may well recall gymkhanas being put on in the area by men from "C" Company.

4. "D" Company was formed in May 1940 starting in Wallasey Village and later moving to "Stoneycroft" Penkett Road. In August 1944 it was merged with "A" Company and became responsible for the administration and training of the "Battle Company". The C.O. was Capt. G.H. Brown who was succeeded by Major J. Howie M.C.

5. "E" Company consisted of a number of detachments involved with some vital projects, for instance, they had a Cycle Platoon, possibly the first in the country. This Company's base was at the School of Art in Central Park with Major Boucher in command. The group excelled in street fighting and shooting, which was due to the use of a convenient indoor rifle range, which was the pride of the men.

The roles of the Companies varied and from the beginning, when recruits were inexperienced and badly equipped, there arose the Home Guard, well trained, with determination and considerable fire power.

Throughout the Borough there were observation posts and road blocks which barred the way to certain areas. These were manned by the Home Guard who stopped passers-by and demanded identity cards. All-night shifts were relieved by jugs of something hot from kind neighbours until dawn came when it was time tor home and a day's work at the office. Beaches were patrolled nightly in case of enemy landings by sea. There was also a mine watching service, a speciality of "E" Company who had Wallasey ferrymen in their ranks excelling in this task. Even fireguard duty was undertaken during the Blitz at public utility places. Training was tested by weekend exercises: in February 1941; May 1942 (code name "Acorn") and September 1942 (code name "Helen").

Operation "Acorn" was a three day, large scale attack with a mock invasion by land sea and air. Home Guards, grim and sooty faced, attacked with Regular Commandos acting as the enemy; they smashed their way into the docks having landed at night in ships in the River; blew up bridges; smashed key points and did untold damage before returning to the ships. Other Home Guards, equally grim, fought on the defending side and were successful at hitting back at the enemy making sure that many never left the docks alive when attack after attack was repulsed. There was hand to hand fighting, grenades, bombs and gas attacks, but all this of course was simulated. Residents were advised to stay at home and those who ventured out without their gas masks returned red eyed and "weeping". An aerial "blitz" was staged which kept the Fire Service and ARP busy. The Police and Civil Defence also played a part as well as the Red Cross and Ambulance to deal with all the casualties. There was even an enemy parachute landing but they were all rounded up by policemen.

A large detachment of Cadets from the 16th Cadet Battalion of the Cheshires did yeoman service as "causalities" and messengers with the catering arrangements, carried out by the W.V.S., being one of the most satisfactory features of the exercise.

Many valuable lessons were learnt from this three day operation, but above all it was the experience of simulated war that was of value to the Home Guard. A similar exercise known as Operation "Helen" was held 19 September 1942 with large forces of enemy parachute troops landing one and a half miles west of Moreton Cross. "C" Company contained most of this enemy force. However, nearly 100 of the enemy escaped and entrenched themselves in Grove Road Station before trying to move into New Brighton. But, of course, the Home Guard saved the day.

Numerous incidents were staged in the Borough. Fires were lit on open spaces and dealt with by the Fire Brigade. High explosives and incendiary bombs were supposed to have been dropped, these being represented by fireworks. The Home Guard Battalion was under the command of Lt. Colonel Duncan Taylor whilst the police and Civil Defence were co-ordinated by Mr John Ormerod the Chief Constable. The idea behind this operation was to test liason between the Army and Civil Defence Services; realism was the keynote.

There were other exercises to test the Home Guard, and in February 1944 there was operation "U.S." with American troops stationed in Wallasey. There were lectures in anti gas defence, construction of field defences, tank destruction, tank traps, there were anti-tank lines along Telegraph Lane, the Fender, and Wallasey Golf Clubs links area. There were road blocks in Portland Street, Atherton Street, Rowson Street, Victoria Road New Brighton, Sea Road, Egremont Promenade, Leasowe Road, Green Lane and Harrison Drive. There was weapon training, with the Battalion winning many competitions for shooting and street fighting. There was also first aid, drill, P.T. and sentry duty but between all that there was living and working a normal day. The Home Guard had been in existence for four and a half years when the final stand down came in December 1944. The streets were thronged with spectators on 4th December when the 700 strong members of the Wallasey Home Guard marched in procession from the Oval Cricket Ground to the Concert Hall in Manor Road led by the band of Birkenhead NFS. Here the salute was taken by Lt. Colonel L. Mickle M.C. and the Mayor Alderman J. Pennington. Thereafter the march continued back to Oldershaw School where the dispersal took place - it must have been a poignant moment. Mention must be made that on 20 May 1941, which was the first anniversary of the Home Guard, they were given the honour of being guard at Buckingham Palace which was repeated on the same day two years later, in 1943. There are many professional regiments, hundreds of years old, who have never had this honour, yet the Home Guard, only four and a half years old had done this twice .... What a wonderful tribute to a fine set of gentlemen.

Joy Hockey

This is a list of some of the officers of the Wallasey Home Guard

NAME	COY	DATE of Appt.	NAME	COY	DATE of Appt.
Lt Colonel W. Duncan Taylor J.P.	Bn HQ	1.2.41	Lieut B. Greaves	D	3.9.41
Major L. Mickle M.C.	Bn HQ	1.2.41	F.J. McAuley	E	11.10.41
H Politt M.C.	C	1.2.41	J.R. Joynson	Bn HQ	25.10.41
A.T. Ashcroft (MO)	Bn HQ	1.2.41	H.P. Thompson	A	28.10.41
J Boucher	E	1.2.41	G.H. Carter	B	14.11.41
C.E. Balmforth	A	1.8.42	W.J. Galleway	C	14.11.41
T.H. Parsons	B	23.11.42	A.F. Henderson	Bn HQ	14.11.41
J. Howie M.C.	D	25.1.43	E.W. Thomas	E	15.12.41
			T McHarrie	D	20.2.42
Capt E.A. Shacklady A.M.	Bn HQ	1.2.41	F. Heath	E	1.2.41
H.V.P. Thorpe	C	1.2.41	F.L. Moss MM	D	29.6.42
J.O. Broster	B	23.5.41	E. Edwards	E	27.7.42
G.H. Bryans	A	16.6.41	G.G. Colton	Bn HQ	10.9.42
J. Allcorn	D	25.7.41	H. Ingham	B	25.9.42
C. Litt	Bn HQ	3.9.41	J. Lewis	C	25.9.42
J Williams (MO)	Bn HQ	13.12.42	R. Griffiths	C	25.9.42
			A.G. Lockwood	QM E	16.11.42
Lieut G.A. Tyrrell	Bn HQ	1.2.41	N. Bell	Bn HQ	12.11.42
J.W. Dickson	Bn HQ	1.2.41			
R.G. Coulstring	Bn HQ	1.2.41	2nd Lieut C.E. Evans	A	8.9.42
H.S. Oddie	Bn HQ	1.2.41	E.A. Cox	D	15.2.41
A.J. Winstanley	A	1.2.41	W.F. Brogan	A	20.2.42
H.L. Smith QM	A	1.2.41	J.W.Sargeant	D	18.5.42
T.A.N. Jones	B	1.2.41	W.C. Oakley	D	18.5.42
L. Ellison QM	C	1.2.41	J.R.F. Currams	E	18.5.42
J. Browne QM	D	1.2.41	R. Huck	C	18.5.42
F.H. Farrelly	A	1.2.41	W.D. McKinley	B	18.5.42
H.S. Glass	A	1.2.41	C. Highet	B	18.5.42
J.N. Gregory M.C.	B	1.2.41	C.J. Campbell	A	18.5.42
C.W. Moss	B	1.2.41	A. Gibson	A	18.5.42
H.S. Wilding	C	1.2.41	T. Robinson	E	18.5.42
T.A. Clarke	C	1.2.41	H.T.K. Morris	C	28.5.42
W.G. Gleasby	C	1.2.41	S.V. Cottrell	D	9.7.42
J.H. Dalgarno	D	1.2.41	R.S. Moore	E	10.9.42
E.J Goodwin	D	1.2.41	F. Bordley	Bn HQ	10.9.42
H.J. Pownall	C	1.2.41	W.A. Rimmer	Coast Defence	12.2.42
W.E. Leigh	B	1.2.41	J.L. Richardson	Coast Defence	12.2.42
H Ball MM	Bn HQ	1.2.41	C.P. Price QM	B	16.2.42
R.S. Baldwin	E	1.2.41	W.J. Hill	B	20.1.43
P.S. Pennington	A	16.6.41	Other Home Guard members mentioned elsewhere		
B.J. Donavon	Bn HQ	24.7.41	G. Thomas W Tyrer C.R. Ambler J Evans		
R.V. Newall	E	15.8.41	G. Williams G Davis F Whitely		

There is a photograph of the Wallasey Home Guard officers on the back cover

LIST of CIVILIANS WHO LOST THEIR LIVES in the COUNTY BOROUGH of WALLASEY 1940-41

THE DUTY OF RECORDING THE NAMES OF THE CIVILIAN WAR DEAD OF THE BRITISH, COMMONWEALTH AND EMPIRE WAS ENTRUSTED BY ROYAL CHARTER IN FEBRUARY 1941, TO THE IMPERIAL WAR GRAVES COMMISSION.

THIS ROLL OF HONOUR IS OF THOSE CIVILIANS WHO WERE KILLED IN THE BOROUGH OF WALLASEY, WHILE ENGAGED IN HOUSEHOLD OR IN BUSINESS ACTIVITIES, OR AT THEIR POSTS AS MEMBERS OF THE CIVIL DEFENCE SERVICES.

There is a special Memorial Case containing the six volumes of the Roll of Honour. One volume lies open so that a double page of names may be read. Above it is a light which is kept burning and a page is turned each day.

ALLDRITT, CATHERINE MAY, age 64, of 4A Bell Road. Daughter of the late Robert and Susan Sanderson, of Liverpool; widow of Joseph Alexander Alldritt. Injured 31 August 1940, at 4A Bell Road; died 2 September 1940, at Victoria Central Hospital.

ANDREW, ETHEL, age 34; of Edenhurst, Atherton Street, New Brighton. Wife of Frederick Stanley Andrew. 9 January 1941, at Edenhurst, New Brighton.

ANDREW, FREDERICK STANLEY, age 34: of Edenhurst, Atherton Street, New Brighton. Son of Thomas G. Andrew, of 16 Karslake Road, Liverpool; husband of Ethel Andrew. 9 January 1941, at Edenhurst, New Brighton.

ARMSTRONG, LILIAN MINNIE, age 64; of 231 Seabank Road. Daughter of W. Armstrong. 23 December 1940, at 231 Seabank Road.

ARMSTRONG, PERCY, age 61; Air Raid Warden. Son of J.N. Armstrong, of 1 Slyne Road, Lancaster, and of the late M.A., Armstrong; husband of Eveline May Armstrong, of 3 Perrin Road. 12 March 1941, at Leasowe Road.

ARNFIELD, AMY, age 39; of 14 Copeland Street, Hyde. Wife of Paul Mason Arnfield. 12 March 1941, at Poulton Road.

ARNFIELD, ELIZABETH HOUGHTON, age 14; of 14 Copeland Street, Hyde. Daughter of Paul Mason Arnfield and Amy Arnfield. 12 March 1941, at Poulton Road.

ARNFIELD, PAUL MASON, age 40, of 14 Copeland Street, Hyde. Husband of Amy Arnfield. 12 March 1941, at Poulton Road.

ATKISS, FRANCIS JOY, age 35; Hoylake Rescue Service. Husband of Ada Atkiss, of 25 Greenheys Road, Irby, Wirral. 13 March 1941 at, Wallasey Road.

AVERY, AGNES ELLEN, age 24; of 62 Northbrook Road. Daughter of Samuel Murray Wilson and Elizabeth Ellen Wilson; wife of Thomas Edward Avery. 12 March 1941, at 68 Northbrook Road.

BADHAM, MURIEL, age 47; of Fern Noole, Sandrock Road. Wife of William J. Badham. 22 December 1940, at Sandrock Road.

BADHAM, WILLIAM J., age 48; of Fern Noole, Sandrock Road. Husband of Muriel Badham. 22 December 1940, at Sandrock Road.

BAIRD, FREDERICA EMILY ANNIE, age 36; of 16 Asbury Road. Wife of James Henry Baird. 12 March 1941, at 16 Asbury Road.

BAIRD, JAMES HENRY, age 41; of 16 Asbury Road. Son of R. J. and E. Baird, of 35 Oxton Road; husband of Frederica Emily Annie Baird. 12 March 1941, at 16 Asbury Road.

BALL, CONSTANCE MARGARET, age 10; of 6 Rockpoint Avenue. Daughter of John B. and Elsie C. Ball. 21 December 1940, at 6 Rockpoint Avenue.

BALL, DAVID RODNEY, age 7; of 12 Brookway. son of Winifred Ball, and of Albert Edward Ball. 12 March 1941, at 12 Brookway.

BALL, JOHANNA, age 71; of 12 Brookway. Widow of David J. Ball. 12 March 1941, at 12 Brookway.

BALLAS, EDITH AGNES, age 65; of Manor Lodge, Manor Road. 21 December 1940, at Manor Lodge.

BANNER, ELLEN GRAHAM, age 75; of Manor Lodge. Manor Road. Daughter of the late J. R. Banner. 21 December 1940, at Manor Lodge.

BARR, THOMAS, age 53; of 15 Grosvenor Road. 5 May 1941, at Grosvenor Road.

BARROW, SAMUEL, age 67; of 22 Central Park Avenue. Husband of Kate Sinclair Barrow. Injured 14 March 1941, at 22 Central Park Avenue; died 15 March 1941, at Victoria Hospital.

BARRY, EDWARD HENRY, age 33; of 46 Grosvenor Street. Son of Mrs. P. L. Barry, of same address, and of the late P. L. Barry; Husband of Irene Mary Barry, 10 August 1940, at Victoria Central Hospital.

BATTING, GUY, age 57; Air Raid Warden; of 23 The Oval. Son of John and Eleanor Batting, of Devonia, Minehead, Somerset; husband of Sybil Batting. 12 March 1941, at 23 The Oval.

BAXTER, ALICE, age 52; of 9 Erskine Road. 12 March 1941, at 9 Erskine Road.

BEARD, BRENDA, age 49, of 113 Poulton Road. Wife of Herbert Beard. 12 March 1941, at 113 Poulton Road.

BEASLEY, EMMA LOUISA, age 69; of 92 Vaughan Road. Wife of Alfred M. Beasley. Injured 21 December 1940, at 92 Vaughan Road; died same day at Victoria General Hospital.

BEDSON, THOMAS, age 53; of 35 Serpentine Road. Husband of A. Bedson. 22 December 1940, at Leasowe Hospital.

BELLAMY, JOHN FREDERICK, age 4; Son of Mr. and Mrs. F. H. Bellamy, of Storeton, Arrowe Park Road, Upton, Wirral. 12 March 1941, at Mill Lane Hospital.

BELLIS, MARTHA, age 70; of Manor Lodge, Manor Road. Daughter of the late Ezra and Sarah Bellis. 21 December 1940, at Manor Lodge.

BENNION, DAVID RICHARD, age 12 months; of 54 Lancaster Avenue, Liscard. Son of John Richard and Mary Bennion. 12 March 1941, at 54 Lancaster Avenue.

BENNION, DOROTHEA MAY, age 3; of 54 Lancaster Avenue, Liscard. Daughter of John Richard and Mary Bennion. 12 March 1941, at 54 Lancaster Avenue.

BENNION, JOHN RICHARD, age 27; of 54 Lancaster Avenue, Liscard. Son of R.S. and Elizabeth Bennion, of 118 Birkenhead Road, Seacombe; husband of Mary Bennion. 12 March 1941, at 54 Lancaster Avenue.

BENNION, MARY, age 24; of 54 Lancaster Avenue, Liscard. Daughter of James and Lucy Burke, of 2 Thirlmere Street, Liscard; wife of John Richard Bennion. 12 March 1941, at 54 Lancaster Avenue.

BERRY, HERBERT CHARLES, age 55; of 46 Palatine Road. 21 December 1940, at 46 Palatine Road.

BINTLEY, GEORGE HENRY, age 33; A.R.P, Supt. Hoylake Rescue Service. Son of Mrs. M. Bintley, of 3 Lyndhurst Road, Great Meols, Hoylake. 13 March 1941, at 1 Newlands Drive.

BIRCHALL, CLARA, age 61; of 50 Leominster Road. Daughter of the late W. Birchall. 21 December 1940, at 50 Leominster Road.

BIRCHALL, MARGARET, age 41; of 26 Gloucester Road. 12 March 1941, at same address (For **BIRD, MARY ANN**, see **LAVELL, MARY ANN**.)

BOUNDY, ERNEST JOHN, age 39. Son of Frank and Elizabeth Boundy, of Ivy Cottage, West Anstey, South Molton, Devonshire; husband of Frances Boundy, of 24A Leasowe Road, Wallasey Village. 12 March 1941, at Leasowe Road.

BOWDEN, WILLIAM HENRY, age 58; Home Guard. Husband of Mary Bowden, of 9 Margaret Street. 13 March 1941, at Wheatland Lane.

BRADLEY, ISABEL, age 64; of Manor Lodge, Manor Road. Daughter of the late J. Bradley. 21 December 1940, at Manor Lodge.

BRASSEY, VERA, age 29. Daughter of Ethel L. Hignett, of The Laurels, Hoylake Road, Moreton; wife of Thomas Stanley Brassey, of the same address. 21 December 1940, at The Laurels.

BRAYSHAW, GRACE ELIZABETH, age 70; of 56 Manor Road. Wife of John Russell Brayshaw. 20 December 1940, at 56 Manor Road.

BRAYSHAW, GRACE MATILDA age 40; of 56 Manor Road. Daughter of John Russell and Grace Elizabeth Brayshaw. 20 December 1940, at 56 Manor Road.

BRAYSHAW, JOHN RUSSELL, age 69; of 56 Manor Road. Husband of Grace Elizabeth Brayshaw. 20 December 1940, at 56 Manor Road.

BRAYSHAW, MARJORIE, age 42; of 56 Manor Road. Daughter of John Russell and Grace Elizabeth Brayshaw. 20 December 1940, at 56 Manor Road.

BROWN, ELIZA ELLEN, age 74; of 25 Church Street Egremont. 12 March 1941, at 25 Church St.

BRYAN, ELIZABETH, age 81; of 28 Church Street, Egremont. 14 March 1941, at Victoria Central Hospital.

BURGE, MARY ANN age 70; of Manor Lodge, Manor Road. 21 December 1940, at Manor Lodge.

BURKES, PETER DENNIS age 12. Son of Henry Walker Burkes and Lily Burkes, of 5 Kingsmead Rd. 13 March 1941, in minefield, Leasowe Golf Club.

BYRNE, JOHN, age 9. Son of Charles Byrne, of 29 Swan Street, Liverpool. 12 March 1941, at Mill Lane Hospital.

BYRNE, JOSEPH HENRY age 45; of 152 Liscard Road. 12 March 1941, at 152 Liscard Road.

CAIN, MARJORIE, age 28; of 69 Dalmorton Road. Daughter of W. Cain. 20 December 1940, at 69 Dalmorton Road.

CAREY, LAWRENCE, age 44; Merchant Navy; of 6 Lily Grove, 10 August 1940, at Victoria Central Hospital.

CARTER, MARTHA age 55; of 18 Eastcroft Road. Daughter of William Brown, of 42 Clarence Street, Morecambe, Lancashire, and of the late Mrs. Brown; wife of John Carter. Injured 20 December 1940, at 18 Eastcroft Road; died same day at Victoria Central Hospital.

CHALLONER, CYRIL HORSEFALL age 34; of 16 Camsdale Road. Husband of Gladys Challoner. 20 December 1940, at 16 Camsdale Rd.

CHALLONER, GLADYS, age 33; of 16 Camsdale Road. Wife of Cyril Horsefall Challoner. 20 December 1940, at 16 Camsdale Road.

CHALLONER, THELMA age 11; of 16 Camsdale Road. Daughter of Cyril Horsefall Challoner and Gladys Challoner. 20 December 1940, at 16 Camsdale Road.

CHATHAM, ANNIE CLEMENTINA age 79; of 61 Withens Lane. Daughter of R. Chatham. 21 December 1940, at 61 Withens Lane.

CHATHAM, ELLEN age 57; of 61 Withens Lane. Wife of Robert John Chatham. Injured 21 December 1940, at 61 Withens Lane; died 22 December 1940, at Cottage Hospital.

CLARKE, ERNEST age 6 months; of 31 Lily Grove. Son of A.B. Ernest Clarke, Merchant Navy, and of May Clarke. 22 September 1940, at 31 Lily Grove.

CLARKE, MAY, age 30; of 31 Lily Grove. Wife of A.B. Ernest Clarke, Merchant Navy. 22 September 1940, at 31 Lily Grove.

CLARKE, VIOLET, age 3; of 3 Lily Grove. Daughter of A.B. Ernest Clarke, Merchant Navy, and of May Clarke. 22 September 1940, at 31 Lily Grove.

CLARKSON, JAMES, age 76: of 23 Kings Lane, Higher Bebington. 12 March 1941, at City Line Sheds, Dock Road.

CLEATOR, CATHERINE, age 64; of 34 Oarside Drive. Wife of Samuel Ellaby Cleator. 12 March 1941, at 34 Oarside Drive.

CLEATOR, SAMUEL ELLABY, age 66; of 34 Oarside Drive. Husband of Catherine Cleator. 12 March 1941, at 34 Oarside Drive.

CLEWETT, LUCY, age 77; of 2 Field Road. Wife of Thomas Clewett. 12 March 1941, at 2 Field Road.

COCKER, HARRY, age 57; of 42 Rivington Road. Husband of Margaret Cocker. 20 December 1940, at 42 Rivington Road.

COCKER, MARGARET, age 53; of 42 Rivington Road. Wife of Harry Cocker. 20 December 1940, at 42 Rivington Road.

COLLINS, DOROTHY, age 25; of 236 Poulton Road. 20 December 1940, at Clifford Road.

COWAN, ANNIE, age 77; of 13 Bowdon Road. 21 December 1940, at 13 Bowdon Road.

COWLEY, EDNA WORTH, age 66; of 23 Walsingham Road. Daughter of the late J. Cowley. 21 December 1940, at 23 Walsingham Road.

CRAIG, ELEANOR, age 76; of 4 Field Road. 2 March 1941, at 2 Field Road.

CRAIG, NORAH, age 41; of 4 Field Road. 12 March 1941, at 2 Field Road.

CROFT, THOMAS, age 54. Husband of Elsie Ann Croft, of 43 Lancaster Avenue. 12 March 1941, at 43 Lancaster Avenue.

CUNNINGHAM, ARTHUR BENJAMIN, age 76: Fire-watcher; of 28 School Lane. Husband of Edith Ann Cunningham. 12 March 1941, at, 8 School Lane.

DALY, BEATRICE STOWELL, age 62; of 23 Church Street. Wife of Leonard Daly. 12 March 1941, at 23 Church Street.

DAVIES, FANNY, age 33; of 24 Leyburn Road. Daughter of Mr. and Mrs. I. Solomon, of 2 Raymond Road; wife of Benjamin Davies. Injured 21 December 1940, at 24 Leyburn Road; died 22 December 1941, at Leasowe Hospital.

DAVIES, MALCOLM, age 2; of 24 Leyburn Road. Son of Benjamin Davies, and of Fanny Davies. 21 December 1940, at 24 Leyburn Road.

DAWSON, ANN, age 33; of 52 Lancaster Avenue. Daughter of S. and M.E. Fawdry, of 19 Beechcroft Road; wife of William Albert Dawson. 12 March 1941, at 52 Lancaster Avenue.

DAWSON, JOHN, age 3; of 52 Lancaster Avenue. Son of William Albert and Ann Dawson. 12 March 1941, at 52 Lancaster Avenue.

DAWSON, WILLIAM ALBERT, age 39; of 52 Lancaster Avenue. Husband of Ann Dawson. 12 March 1941, at 52 Lancaster Avenue.

DAY, NOEL RICHARD, age 40; F.A.P. Ambulance Driver. Son of the late Charles Henry and Sarah Day; husband of Anne Day, of 5 Lindeth Avenue. 13 March 1941, at Central Park Recreation Ground.

DEAN, NORMAN WILLIS, age 18; of 66 Serpentine Road. Son of Mr. H. H. Dean. 21 December 1940, at 66 Serpentine Road.

DEARING, PERCY, age 27; Fireman, A.F.S.; of 27 The Grove. 20 December 1940, at Electrical Works, Limekiln Lane.

DENVIR, ELSIE JOSEPHINE, age 38; of 54 Manor Road. Wife of P.J. Denvir. 20 December 1940, at 54 Manor Road.

DERWENT, MARY AGNES, age 62; of 70 Marlowe Road. Widow of Thomas Derwent. 12 March 1941, at 70 Marlowe Road.

DICKINSON, JESSIE, age 50; of 25 Harrow Road. Wife of H. W. Dickinson. 12 March 1941, at 25 Harrow Road.

DICKINSON, JOSEPH, age 58; Steward, Merchant Navy; of 31 Ivor Road. 12 March 1941, at Poulton Road.

DODD, JAMES ALEXANDER, age 32; of 60 Norwood Road. Husband of May Dodd. 13 March 1941, at Norwood Road.

DODD, MAY, age 30; of 60 Norwood Road. Wife of James Alexander Dodd. Injured 13 March 1941, at Norwood Road; died 14 March 1941, at Victoria Central Hospital.

DOYLE, SIMON, age 61; Firewatcher. Husband of Catherine Doyle, of 13 Gillbrook Square, Birkenhead. 12 March 1941, at City Line Sheds, Seacombe.

DUKE, MARY LELLA, age 22. Daughter of Mrs. M. E. Duke, of 19 Fairview Avenue. Injured 13 March 1941, at Harrow Road; died same day at Victoria Central Hospital.

DUNN, AMELIA, age 48; of 28 Coningsby Drive. Widow of J. C. Dunn, died 19 October 1940, at 28 Coningsby Drive.

DYSON, HERBERT SEARL, age 59; of 28 Winchester Drive. 12 March 1941, at 28 Winchester Drive.

EDWARDS, GERTRUDE ELIZABETH, age 48; of 20 Leasowe Road. Wife of William Leonard Edwards. 12 March 1941, at 20 Leasowe Road.

EDWARDS, HERBERT, age 46; of 34 Leasowe Road Son of the late George and Jane Edwards, of Liverpool; husband of Alice Edwards. 12 March 1941, at 34 Leasowe Road.

EDWARDS, JOYCE ELIZABETH, age 11; of 20 Leasowe Road. Daughter of William Leonard Edwards, and of Gertrude Elizabeth Edwards. 12 March 1941, at 20 Leasowe Road.

EVANS, CHARLES PERCY, age 57; of 90 Claremount Road. Husband of Nellie Florence Evans. 12 March 1941, at 90 Claremount Road.

EVANS, FRANK, age 32. Son of William Charles Evans, of 44 St. Andrews Road, Bebington. 21 December 1940, at Grove Road.

EVANS, NELLIE FLORENCE, age 58; of 90 Claremount Road. Wife of Charles Percy Evans. 12 March 1941, at 90 Claremount Road.

FAIRCLOUGH, GEORGE ROBERT, age 52. Husband of L. Fairclough, of 20 Sutton Road. 21 December 1940, at Victoria Central Hospital.

FAULKNER, IDA AGNES, age 72; of 59 Church Street, Egremont. Widow of Samuel Faulkner. 12 March 1941, at 59 Church Street.

FAULKNER, LILIAN MAY, age 52; of 59 Church Street, Egremont. Daughter of Ida Agnes, and of the late Samuel Faulkner. 12 March 1941, at 59 Church Street.

FELLOWS, GERALD FRANCIS, age 18; of 58 Lancaster Avenue. Son of Jane Fellows, and of the late Harry Fellows. 12 March 1941, at 58 Lancaster Avenue.

FERNIE, SARAH, age 56; of 78 Urmson Road Widow of J. Fernie. 20 December 1940, at 78 Urmson Road.

FIDLER, GEORGE, age 38; of 7 The Grove, Poulton. Husband of Lilian Fidler. 13 March 1941, at 7 The Grove.

FIDLER, JEAN, age 4. Daughter of John and Edna Fidler, of 87 Liscard Road. 13 March 1941, at Brentwood Street.

FIDLER, STEWART, age 6. Daughter of John and Edna Fidler, of 87 Liscard Road. 13 March 1941, at Brentwood Street.

FIELDEN, SARAH ANN, age 72; of 45 Dawlish Road. 20 December 1941 at 45 Dawlish Road.

FINN, ERNEST GEORGE, age 25; of 71 Dalmorton Road. Husband of Winifred Finn. 20 December 1940, at 71 Dalmorton Road.

FINN, GEORGE, age 11 months; of 71 Dalmorton Road. Son of Ernest George and Winifred Finn. 20 December 1940, at 71 Dalmorton Road.

FINN, WINIFRED, age 27; of 71 Dalmorton Road. Wife of Ernest George Finn. 20 December 1940, at 71 Dalmorton Road.

FINNEY, JAMES ROY, age 36; of 32 Cardigan Street, Birkenhead. Son of James Hall Finney, of 130 Argyle Street South, Birkenhead; husband of Beatrice Finney. 12 March 1941, at Leasowe Road.

FIRTH, RITA MARGARET, age 19; W.V.S.; of 18 Asbury Road. Daughter of Laurence and Ellen Jean Firth. 12 March 1941, at 18 Asbury Road.

FITZPATRICK, ANNIE, age 75; 17 Dovedale Road. Widow of P. Fitzpatrick. 20 December 1940, at 17 Dovedale Road.

FORD, MARGARET, age 34; of 17 Church Street, Egremont. Wife of M. Ford. 12 March 1941, at 17 Church Street.

FORD, MICHAEL, age 17 months; of 17 Church Street, Egremont. Son of M. Ford, and of Margaret Ford. 12 March 1941, at 17 Church Street.

FRANKLIN, ADA, age 52; of 88 Kingsway. Wife of Rupert Franklin. 22 December 1940, at 88 Kingsway.

FRANKLIN, DAISY CHRISTINA, age 20; of 88 Kingsway. Daughter of Rupert and Ada Franklin. 22 December 1940, at 88 Kingsway.

FRANKLIN, RUPERT, age 55; of 88 Kingsway. Husband of Ada Franklin. 22 December 1940, at 88 Kingsway.

FREEMAN, LOUIS, age 37; of 18 Clarence Street, Liverpool. 20 December 1940, at Harrison Drive Shelter.

FRENCH, ERIC WILLIAM, age 30; of 28 Lancaster Avenue. Husband of Winifred French. 12 March 1941, at 28 Lancaster Avenue.

GABB, EDWIN JOHN, age 22; Merchant Navy; of 4 Lily Grove, 10 August 1940, at Victoria Central Hospital.

GAUNT, CHARLOTTE ALICE, age 60; of 8 Hillside Road. Wife of G. Gaunt. Injured 20 December 1940, at 8 Hillside Road; died same day at Victoria Central Hospital.

GEE, JUNG (otherwise **GEE, HARRY**), age 53; of 149 Borough Road. 12 March 1941, at 149 Borough Road.

GIBSON, SIDNEY, age 29; of 42 Lancaster Avenue. Son of William Grindley Gibson and Annie Agnes Gibson, of 6 Withensfield; husband of Cissy Gibson. 12 March 1941, at 42 Lancaster Avenue.

GREGORY, BRIAN JAMES, age 22 months; of 42 Rivington Road. Son of Frank James Gregory, and of Edna Gregory. 20 December 1940, at 42 Rivington Road.

GREGORY, EDNA, age 29; of 42 Rivington Road. Wife of Frank James Gregory. 20 December 1940, at 42 Rivington Road.

GRIFFITHS, ANNIE JANE MAY, age 60, of 21 Walsingham Road. Wife of George Griffiths. 21 December 1940, at 21 Walsingham Road.

GRIFFITHS, GEORGE, age 58; of 21 Walsingham Road. Husband of Annie Jane May Griffiths. 21 December 1940, at 21 Walsingham Road.

GRISDALE, WILLIAM WALTER, age 67; Air Raid Warden; Firewatcher. Husband of S. Grisdale, of 27 Sandcliffe Road. 13 March 1941, at Marks and Spencer's Building.

HALLIDAY, EMMA, age 69; of 9 The Village. 13 March 1941, at 9 The Village.

HAMPSON, HENRIETTA, age 77; of Manor Lodge, Manor Road. 21 December 1940, at Manor Lodge.

HANSON, CHARLES HAROLD, age 42; of 45 Wheatland Lane. Son of the late William and Ellen Hanson, of 33 Wheatland Lane; husband of Elinor Hanson. 13 March 1941, at 45 Wheatland Lane.

HANSON, PETER DANIEL, age 8. Son of Mr. and Mrs. James William Hanson, of 11 The Avenue, New Brighton. 23 December 1940, at Victoria Road, New Brighton.

HARRISON, GEORGE, age 39; Fireman, A.F.S. Husband of C. H. Harrison, of 23 Ivor Road. 13 March 1941, at Cottage Hospital.

HEATON, EDNA EVELYN, age 29 of 32 Merton Road. Wife of Robert Campbell Heaton. 21 December 1940, at Grove Road.

HIGGINS, PATRICK, age 41; Firewatcher; of 88 Claremount Road. Son of Patrick and Catherine Higgins, of 31 Dalmorton Road; husband of Nora Higgins. 12 March 1941, at Claremount Road.

HIPKISS, DEREK HEATH, age 2; of 42 Rivington Road. Son of Mne. Thomas Hipkiss, Royal Marines, and Elsie Hipkiss. 20 December 1940, at 42 Rivington Road.

HOLDEN, GEORGE, age 39; of 34A Church Street, Egremont. Husband of Phyllis Holden. 12 March 1941, at 34A Church Street.

HOLROYD, ELLLEN, age 67; of 77 Wallasey Village. Widow of John E. Holroyd. 12 March 1941, at 83 Wallasey Village.

HOLROYD, MARTHA, age 43; of 77 Wallasey Village. Daughter of Ellen and of the late John E. Holroyd. 12 March 1941, at 83 Wallasey Village.

HOPKINS, WILLIAM, age 64; Home Guard; of 4 Heathbank Avenue. Husband of Margaret Hopkins. 21 December 1940, at 4 Heathbank Ave.

HOUNSOME, BERTHA MAUD, age 70; of 25 Church Street, Egremont. 12 March 1941, at 25 Church St.

HOWARD, CHARLES, age 76; of 95 Rowson Street. Husband of Esther Howard, 1 November 1940, at 95 Rowson Street.

HOWARD, ESTHER, age 70; of 95 Rowson Street. Wife of Charles Howard, 1 November 1940, at 95 Rowson Street.

HUGHES, EDWARD HERBERT, age 70; of 90 Penkett Road. 21 December 1940, at 90 Penkett Road.

HUGHES, FLORENCE EDITH, age 24; of 9 St. Albans Road. Daughter of Mr. G.F. Light, of 9 Tower Street; wife of Albert Alan Hughes. Injured 12 March 1941, at 9 St. Albans Road; died 13 March 1941, at Victoria Central Hospital.

HUGHES, GEORGE, age 3; of 9 St. Albans Road. Son of Albert Alan Hughes, and of Florence Edith Hughes. 12 March 1941, at 9 St. Albans Road.

HUGHES, KENNETH STEVEN, age 6 months; of 9 St. Albans Road. Son of Albert Alan Hughes, and of Florence Edith Hughes. 12 March 1941 at 9 St. Albans Road.

HUGHES, LEONARD JOSEPH, age 19. Son of Frederick Hughes, of 57 Baden Road, Old Swan, Liverpool. 12 March 1941. at 15 Erskine Road.

HUGHES MEURIG, age 20; of 44 Rufford Road. Son of Mr & Mrs Meurig Hughes, of Acrefair, Wrexham, North Wales. 12 March 1941, at Poulton Road.

HUGHES, RHODA, age 41; of 181 Wheatland Lane. Daughter of the late Rowland Hughes. 10 August 1940, at 181 Wheatland Lane.

HUGHES, ROBERT BRISTOW, age 72; of 90 Penkett Road. 21 December 1940, at 90 Penkett Road.

HUNTINGTON, ANDREW, age 85; of 11 St. Albans Road. Injured 12 March 1941, at 11 St. Albans Rd; died 14 March 1941, at Victoria Central Hospital.

HUNTINGTON, JOHN, age 17 Son of John and Mary Huntington, of 27 Stonehouse Road. 12 March 1941, at 11 St. Albans Road.

HURST, JESSICA MAY, age 39; of 5 St. Mary's Ave. Daughter of Lily Hurst, and of the late John Henry Hurst. 12 March 1941, at 5 St. Mary's Avenue.

HUSTON, WILLIAM, age 45; of 3 Adelaide Street, 10 August 1940, at 7 Adelaide Street.

JACK, GERTRUDE, age 50; of Daresbury Road. Daughter of Sarah Melville Jack, and of the late George Jack. 12 March 1941, at 1 Daresbury Road

JACK, LILIAN, age 60; of 1 Daresbury Road. Daughter of Sarah Melville Jack, and of the late George Jack. 12 March 1941, at 1 Daresbury Rd.

JACK, SARAH MELVILLE, age 84; of Daresbury Road. Widow of George Jack. 12 March 1941, at 1 Daresbury Road.

JAMES, ALBERT CHARLES, age 36; A.R.P.; A.F.S.; of 30 Briardale Road. Husband of Mary James. 22 September 1940, at 30 Briardale Road.

JARRETT, WILLIAM MICHAEL, age 52; of 47 Stringhey Road 19 October 1940, at 28 Coningsby Drive.

JEFFERSON, JAMES, age 72; Air Raid Warden; of 20 Clifford Road. 12 March 1941, at Erskine Road.

JENNINGS, KATHLEEN, age 19; of 15 Erskine Road. Daughter of William, and Sarah Jennings. 12 March 1941, at 15 Erskine Road.

JENNINGS, LAVINIA ELIZABETH, age 13; of 15 Erskine Road. Daughter of William and Sarah Jennings. 12 March 1941, at 15 Erskine Road.

JENNINGS, MARGARET, age 16; of 15 Erskine Road. Daughter of William and Sarah Jennings. 12 March 1941, at 15 Erskine Road.

JENNINGS, SARAH, age 50; of 15 Erskine Road. Wife of William Jennings. 12 March 1941, at 15 Erskine Road.

JENNINGS, WILLIAM, age 50; Firewatcher; of 15 Erskine Road. Husband of Sarah Jennings. 12 March 1941; at 15 Erskine Road.

JOHNSTON, JOHN HAROLD, age 26; of 35 Erskine Road. Son of Joseph, and E. Johnston. 13 March 1941, at Central Park Recreation Ground.

JONES, ALICE, age 85; of 5 St. Mary's Avenue. 12 March 1941, at St. Mary's Avenue.

JONES, PETER LANGLEY, age 58. Husband of Elizabeth Jones, of 15 Glyn Road. 12 March 1941, at Buchanan's Mill.

KELLAND, AMY SPENCE, age 51; of 10 Lyncroft Road. Daughter of the late Charles and Harriet Walker, of 24 Bridge Road, Liverpool; widow of Edmund Kelland. 12 March 1941, at Poulton Road.

KELLY, CATHERINE LILIAN, age 14; of 11 St. Albans Road. Daughter of Denis and Margaret Kelly.. Injured 12 March 1941, at 11 St. Albans Road; died 14 March 1941, at Victoria Central Hospital.

KENDRICK, FLORENCE ETHEL, age 59; Of 9 Mere Lane. Wife of Thomas Herbert Kendrick. 14 March 1941, at 9 Mere Lane.

KENDRICK, THOMAS HERBERT, age 62; of 9 Mere Lane. Husband of Florence Ethel Kendrick. 14 March 1941, at 9 Mere Lane.

KNIGHT, EDWARD HORACE, age 30; of 31 Vyner Rd. Son of Mr. and Mrs. Edward Knight, of 49 Dereham Rd., Barking, Essex; husband of Marjorie Wendy Knight. Injured 1 November 1941, at 31 Vyner Rd; died same day at Victoria Central Hospital

KNIGHT, FLORENCE MARY, age 69; of Manor Lodge, Manor Road. Daughter of T.J. Knight. 21 December 1940, at Manor Lodge.

KNIGHT, MARJORIE WENDY, age 32; of 31 Vyner Road. Daughter of Beatrice Torkildsen, of 20 Wolseley Road, Forest Gate, London, and of the late Oscar F. Torkildsen; wife of Edward Horace Knight. Injured 1 November 1941, at 31 Vyner Road; died 2 November 1941, at Victoria Central Hospital.

LAMONT, MAUD MARY, age 58; of 5 Newton Road. Widow of Archibald Lament. 13 March 1941, at 5 Newton Road.

LATHAM, MARY ANN, age 79. 12 March 1941, at 59 Church Street, Egremont.

LAUDER, ALFRED SHARPLES, age 38; Decontamination Service: of 59 Wheatland Lane. Husband of Emma Owen Lauder. 13 March 1941, at 41 Wheatland Lane.

LAVELL (otherwise BIRD), MARY ANN, age 85; of 25 Church Street, Egremont. Widow of M. Lavell. 12 March 1941, at 25 Church Street.

LAWSON, JOHN DOLLAWAY, age 40; Home Guard; of 56 Wheatland Lane. Son of the late John Thomas and Martha Lawson; of 35 Crosthwaite Avenue, Eastham, Wirral; husband of Vera Lawson. Injured 13 March 1941, at 56 Wheatland Lane; died same day at Victoria Central Hospital.

LAWTON, ROBERT MURRAY, age 52; of 19 Dovedale Road. 20 December 1940, at 19 Dovedale Road.

LEARY, EVELYN MURIEL, age 8. Daughter of Mr. A. Leary, of 10 Erskine Road. 13 March 1941, at Victoria Central Hospital.

LEIGH, FLORENCE, age 42; of 18 Carnsdale Road. Wife of H. T. V. Leigh. 20 December 1940, at 18 Carnsdale Road.

LEIGH, PAMELA FLORENCE, age 12; of 18 Carnsdale Road. Daughter of H. T. V. Leigh, and of Florence Leigh. 20 December 1940, at 18 Carnsdale Road.

LEWIS, FRANCES MAY, age 59; of 46 St. George's Road. Widow of James Seatey Lewis. 12 March 1941; at Pensioners Cottages, School Lane.

LICKFOLD, ENID FRANCES, age 25; of 5 Sandy Lane. Wife of D. Lickfold. 12 March 1941, at 6 Sandy Lane.

LITTLE, ADA HARRIET, age 60; of 34 Kinnaird Road. 22 December 1940, at 34 Kinnaird Road.

LITTLE, ELSIE, age 47; of 20 School Lane. Daughter of the late Henry and Harriet Webster; widow of Frank Little. 12 March 1941, at School Lane.

McDONALD, JAMES, age 39; F.A.P. Member; of 55 Wheatland Lane. Son of James and Margaret McDonald. 13 March 1941, at Cross Street.

McGREGOR, ANNIE, age 48; of 37 Serpentine Road. Widow of C. McGregor. 21 December 1940, at 37 Serpentine Road.

McGREGOR, BRIAN, age 14; of 37 Serpentine Road. Son of Annie and of the late C. McGregor. 21 December 1940, at 37 Serpentine Road.

McGREGOR, EILEEN, age 17; of 37 Serpentine Road. Daughter of Annie and of the late C. McGregor. 21 December 1940, at 37 Serpentine Road.

McNALLY, GERTRUDE, age 38; B.R.C.S.; of 34 Oarside Drive. Daughter of the late Patrick and Anne McNally, of 101 Barrington Road, Wavertree, Liverpool. 12 March 1941, at 34 Oarside Drive.

MADDOCK, WILLIAM WALLACE, age 37; of 6 Erskine Road. 12 March 1941, at Erskine Road.

MADDOX, CHARLES EDWARD, age 57; F.A.P. member of 10 Tiverton Avenue. Husband of Louisa Maud Maddox. 4 May 1946, at 10 Tiverton Avenue.

MAINWARING, WILLIAM THOMAS, age 20; 25 Hawthorndale Road. Son of Thomas William Mainwaring, and of the late Margaret Helen Mainwaring. 12 March 1941, at 25 Hawthorndale Rd

MARRIOTT, ARTHUR SPYZER, age 35; of 50 Lancaster Avenue. Son of Arthur and Edith Annie Marriott, of 43 Geneva Road; husband of Jenny Marriott. 12 March 1941, at 50 Lancaster Avenue.

MARRIOTT, JENNY, age 33; of 50 Lancaster Avenue. Daughter of John and Mary Burkey, "The Bungalow" Heathfield, Heath Lane, Willaston; wife of Arthur Spyzer Marriott, 12 March 1941 at 50 Lancaster Avenue.

MARTIN, ARTHUR, age 44; of 36 Kinnaird Road. 22 December 1940, at 36 Kinnaird Road.

MARTLEW, NORAH EVELYN, age 47. Daughter of Charles F. and Esther Howard; wife of Robert Martlew, of 95 Rowson Street, 1 November 1940, at 95 Rowson Street.

MAXFIELD, JOHN THOMAS, age 65; of 8 Byron Road. 13 March 1941 at Wheatland Lane.

MEALOR, HAROLD, age 34; Firewatcher; of 8 Foxhey Road. Son of Howard Mealor, of 34 Inglemere Road, Rock Ferry, Birkenhead, and of the late H. Mealor; husband of Florida May Mealor. 12 March 1941, at 8 Foxhey Road.

MOORE, CHARLES LESLIE, age 64; of 92 Claremount Road. Husband of Mary Emily Moore. 12 March 1941, at Claremount Road.

MOORE, MARY EMILY, age 69; of 92 Claremount Road. Wife of Charles Leslie Moore. 12 March 1941, at Claremount Road.

MUNCE, HARRIET LOUISA, age 59; of 26 Gloucester Road. Daughter of the late Walter Thomas and Emma Elizabeth Finch, of 60 Edge Grove, Fairfield, Liverpool; wife of Thomas Ernest Munce. 12 March 1941; at 26 Gloucester Road.

MUNCE, THOMAS ERNEST, age 59; of 26 Gloucester Road. Husband of Harriet Louisa Munce. 12 March 1941, at 26 Gloucester Road

MURPHY, JOHN, age 40; of 44 Reeds Avenue. 12 March 1941, at Reeds Avenue.

MURPHY, JOHN, age 10; of 10 Plumton St. Everton, Liverpool. 13 April 1941, at Leasowe Sandhills.

NIELD, HILDA MARY, age 38; of 62 Norwood Road. Daughter of the late John and Phoebe Young Salkeld; wife of Syrald Nield. 13 March 1941, at 62 Norwood Road.

NIELD, SYRALD, age 37; of 62 Norwood Road. Son of Mary Nield, of Huxley; husband of Hilda Mary Nield. 13 March 1941, at 62 Norwood Road.

NOBLE, EILEEN, age 7; of 149 Borough Road. Daughter of Harriet Noble. 12 March 1941; at. 149 Borough Road.

NOSCOE, MARY ELLEN, age 57; Daughter of J. Noscoe, of Manor Lodge, Manor Road. 21 December 1940, at Manor Lodge.

OLDFIELD, MARY, age 48; of 11 Asbury Road. Wife of Walter Oldfield. 12 March 1941, at 16 Asbury Rd

OLDFIELD, WALTER, age 48; of 11 Asbury Road. Husband of Mary Oldfield. 12 March 1941, at 16 Asbury Road.

PAPPIN, ETHEL, age 55; A.R.P. Control Service; of 6 Manor Lane. Daughter of Benjamin and Sarah Whalley, of Littledale Road; wife of Charles Richard Pappin. 21 December 1940, at 61 Withens Lane.

PARKER, MRS., age 76; of 25 Church Street, Egremont. 12 March 1941, at 25 Church Street.

PARKER, JAMES, age 67; Firewatcher. Husband of Elizabeth Parker, of 15 Tweed Street. 12 March 1941, at City Line Sheds, Dock Road.

PATERSON, ROBERT SMITH, age 59; of 55 Lancaster Avenue. Husband of Ethel Stewart Paterson. 12 March 1941, at Lancaster Avenue.

PEERS, MARY ANN, age 69; of 28 St. Albans Road. 12 March 1941, at St. Albans Road.

PETRIE, EDITH ANNIE, age 68; of 34 Kinnaird Road. Daughter of the late Mr. and Mrs. Little, of Breck Road, Anfield, Liverpool; widow of George Petrie. Injured 22 December 1940, at 34 Kinnaird Road; died same day at Leasowe Hospital.

POTTER, JANET, age 80; of 58 Manor Road. Widow of Capt. Thomas Potter. 20 December 1940, at 58 Manor Road.

PRESTON, WILLIAM, age 70; of 1 Backwater Street, Egremont. Husband of Theresa Preston. 4 May 1941, at 1 Backwater Street.

RAE, WILLIAM COLIN, age 51; Air Raid Warden; of 36 Clifford Road. Husband of Ethel Rae. 12 March 1941, at 36 Clifford Road.

RAMSAY, ALEXANDER, age 50; of 58 Manor Road. Son of the late James and Elizabeth Ramsay; husband of Frances Margaret Ramsay. 20 December 1940, at 58 Manor Road.

RAMSDEN, HELEN, age 7 months; of 6 Brockley Ave Daughter of P. Ramsden and of Olive Christine Ramsden. 21 December 1940, at Brockley Avenue.

RAMSDEN, KATHLEEN, age 51; of 6 Brockley Avenue. Widow of W. F. Ramsden. 21 December 1940, at Brockley Avenue.

RAMSDEN, OLIVE CHRISTINE, age 20; of 6 Brockley Avenue. Wife of P. Ramsden. 21 December 1940, at Brockley Avenue.

RAMSDEN, PAUL, age 2; of 6 Brockley Avenue. Son of P. Ramsden and of Olive Christine Ramsden. 21 December 1940, at Brockley Avenue.

RAYNER, DAVID JOHN, age 50; for 30 years devoted to the welfare of the crippled children of Stepney and Mile End. Husband of Gwen Rayner, of 28 Weigall Road, Lee, London. 21 December 1940, at 81 Rowson Street.

RICHINGS, ERNEST, age 30: Fireman, A.F.S. Son of Mr. and Mrs. E. J. Richings, of 3 Brookway; husband of Ethel Phyllis Richings, of 55 Vyner Road. 12 March 1941, at Poulton Road.

ROBERTS, JOHN, age 55; of 175 Pit Lane, Birchfield Road, Widnes, Lancashire. 12 March 1941, at City Line Sheds, Dock Road.

ROBERTS, THOMAS HENRY, age 33; Fireman, A.F.S. Son of William Edward and Annie Roberts, of 56 Byerley Street; husband of Ada Roberts, of 18 Wimbledon Street. Injured 13 March 1941, at Lancaster Ave; died same day at Cottage Hospital.

ROBINSON, DESMOND CAUNCE, age 13. Son of Charles Henry and Ethel Robinson, of 3 Birket Close, Leasowe. 13 March 1941, in minefield, Leasowe Golf Club.

ROGERS, MARGARET, age 36. Daughter of Charles and Florence Rogers, of 32 Danehurst Road. Injured 20 December 1940, at Harrison Drive; died 22 December 1940, at Leasowe Hospital.

ROGERSON, WILLIAM, age 37; Fireman, A.F.S. Husband of Margaret Rogerson, of 4 Fell Brow, Longridge, Preston, Lancashire. 18 March 1941, at East Float Docks.

ROSS, EMMA, age 73; of 23 Walsingham Road. Widow of F. Ross. 21 December 1940, at Walsingham Road.

ROWLANDS, GEORGE, age 50. Husband of Ethel Rowlands, of 17 Chapelhill Road, Moreton. Injured 22 December 1940, at 17 Chapelhill Rd; died same day at Leasowe Hospital.

SANDERSON, BERTHA, age 34; L.T.C.L. Daughter of John Sanderson, of 24. Moorcroft Road, and of the late Mary J. Sanderson. 20 December 1940, at Manor Road.

SAVAGE, FLORENCE ELIZABETH GERTRUDE, age 32. Daughter of William and Sarah Savage, of 34 Stonehouse Road. 12 March 1941, at School Lane.

SAWYER, MARGARET ELIZA, age 79; of Manor Lodge, Manor Road. Widow of W. Sawyer. 21 December 1940, at Manor Lodge.

SELBY, ANNIE FRANCIS, Aged 23; of 113 Poulton Road. Daughter of William and Ruth Selby. 12 March 1941, at 113 Poulton Road.

SERVANTIE, PAUL JEAN, age 55. Husband of L. Servantie, of 5 Springvale. 21 December 1940, at Leasowe Hospital.

SHARPE, FLORENCE, age 68; of 4 Evesham Road. Wife of Frank Albert Sharpe. 12 March 1941, at 2 Evesham Road.

SHARPE, FRANK ALBERT, age 72; of 4 Evesham Road. Husband of Florence Sharpe. 12 March 1941, at 2 Evesham Road.

SHAW, JOHN HENRY GEORGE VERNON, age 53. of 7 Palmerston Road. Husband of Mabel Shaw. Injured 21 December 1940, at Palmerston Road; died 24 December 1940, at Leasowe Hospital.

SHAW, MABEL, age 44; of 7 Palmerston Road. Wife of John Henry George Vernon Shaw. Injured 21 December 1940, at Palmerston Road; died 30 December 1940, at Leasowe Hospital.

SHAW, MARGERY MAY, age 16; of 7 Palmerston Road. Daughter of John Henry George Vernon Shaw and Mabel Shaw. 21 December 1940, at Palmerston Road.

SHERIDAN, CATHERINE ROBINA, age 41; Air Raid Warden; of 18 Leasowe Road. 12 March 1941, at Leasowe Road.

SHORT, JAMES HENRY, age 70; of 150 Mill Lane. 10 August 1940, at 150 Mill Lane.

SIMONDS, BARTLE AUGUSTUS, age 52; of 13 Bowdon Road. Son of Richard Charles and Annie Simonds, of 55 Aireville Road, Frizinghall, Bradford, Yorkshire; husband of Mabel Simonds. 21 December 1940, at 13 Bowdon Road.

SIMONDS, MABEL, age 45; of 13 Bowdon Road. Daughter of Annie and of the late Mr. Cowan; wife of Bartle Augustus Simonds.; 21 December 1940, at 13 Bowdon Road.

SMART, DOREEN, age 19; of 14 Radnor Drive. Daughter of Ruby Smart, and of the late J. Smart. 21 December 1940, at Rowson Street.

SMART, RUBY, age 46; of 14 Radnor Drive. Widow of J. Smart. 21 December 1940, at Rowson Street.

SMITH, CAROLINE JANE, age 71; of Manor Lodge, Manor Road. Daughter of the late S. Smith. 21 December 1940, at Manor Lodge.

SMITH, JOHN FERGUS, age 10. Son of George Reginald and Florence Amy Smith, of 35 Birket Avenue, Leasowe. 13 March 1941, in minefield, Leasowe Golf Club.

SMYTH, WILLIAM JAMES, age 59; Air Raid Warden; of 40 Duke St. 31 May 1941. at St. George's Park.

SNELSON, BESSIE, age 35; of 19 Asbury Road. Daughter of Mr. and Mrs. F. Evans, of 81 Bowden Road, Garston, Liverpool; wife of William Athol Snelson. 12 March 1941, at 19 Asbury Road.

SNELSON, GEORGE FREDERICK ATHOL, age 4; of 19 Asbury Road. Son of William Athol and Bessie Snelson. 12 March 1941; at 19 Asbury Road.

SNELSON, WILLIAM ATHOL, age 34; Special Constable; of 19 Asbury Road. Son of Margaret Jane Snelson, of 17 Devonshire Road, and of the late James Frederick Snelson; husband of Bessie Snelson. 12 March 1941, at 19 Asbury Road.

SPEAKMAN, ROBERT HENRY, age 16. Son of F. Speakman, of 10 Addington Street. 21 December 1940, at Serpentine Road.

STARK, JOAN, age 13; of 8 Florence Road. Daughter of F. W. Stark. 22 December 1940, at 8 Florence Road.

STEAD, JAMES, age 58. Husband of Agnes Stead, of 29 Brentwood Avenue, Liverpool. 1 September 1940, at Victoria Central Hospital.

STEEDMAN, SHEILA, age 7 months. Daughter of S. and J. Steedman, of 5 Windsor Street, New Brighton. 7 May 1941, at 5 Windsor Street.

TAYLOR, MABEL LUCILLE, age 18. Daughter of Mr. W. Taylor, of 37 Birnam Road. 20 December 1940, at Victoria Central Hospital.

THOMAS, GEORGE ERNEST LEONARD, age 29; Air Raid Warden. Son of Mrs. K. Thomas, of 27 Brougham Road, Seacombe, and of the late B.E.M. Thomas. 12 March 1941, at Leasowe Road.

THOMPSON, ISABELLA, age 68; of 22 Withington Road. Wife of William Henry Thompson. 21 December 1940, at 22 Withington Road.

THOMPSON, JOAN ELIZABETH, age 4; of 68 Northbrook Road. Daughter of William Henry and Sarah Louise Thompson. 12 March 1941, at 68 Northbrook Road.

THOMPSON, SARAH LOUISE, age 43; of 68 Northbrook Road. Wife of William Henry Thompson. 12 March 1941, at 68 Northbrook Road.

THOMPSON, WILLIAM HENRY, age 41; of 68 Northbrook Road. Husband of Sarah Louise Thompson. 12 March 1941, at 68 Northbrook Road.

THOMSON, EMILY MABEL, age 47; of 4 Lyndhurst Road. Daughter of the late Frederick and Anne Helena Broadbridge, of Liverpool; wife of William Allan Thomson. 12 March 1941, at Lyndhurst Road.

THOMSON, WILLIAM ALLAN, age 61; Air Raid Warden; of 4 Lyndhurst Road. Son of the late John and Margaret Thomson, of Annan, Scotland; husband of Emily Mabel Thomson. 12 March 1941; at Lyndhurst Road.

THORPE, HERBERT, age 62; Air Raid Warden; of 2 Evesham Rd. Son of the late Alexander and Sarah Jane Thorpe, of Afriton, Prenton, Birkenhead; husband of Amy Thorpe. 12 March 1941, at 2 Evesham Road.

THORPE, MURIEL, age 21; of 2 Evesham Road. Daughter of Amy Thorpe, and of Herbert Thorpe. 12 March 1941, at 2 Evesham Road.

THRELFALL, LILIAN MAY, age 53; of 4 Vaughan Road. Daughter of the late Capt. and Mrs. T. L. Threlfall. Injured 21 December 1940, at 94 Vaughan Rd.; died 22 December 1940, at Leasowe Hospital.

TODD, EVANGELINE, age 24: of 11 Imperial Avenue. 21 December 1940, at 81 Rowson Street.

TOLLIDAY, ETHNE CAROLE, age 14 months; of 17 Asbury Road. Daughter of Norman J. and Vera Tolliday. 12 March 1941, at 17 Asbury Road.

TOWERS, JOSEPH, age 72; of 8 Florence Road. Husband of Sarah Towers. 22 December 1940, at 8 Florence Road.

TOWERS, SARAH, age 71; of 8 Florence Road. Wife of Joseph Towers. 22 December 1940, at 8 Florence Road.

TRAPNELL, CLARA, age 50; of 2 Willoughby Road. Wife of H. H. Trapnell. 13 March 1941, at 2 Willoughby Road.

TRAPNELL, ELSIE, age 24; of 2 Willoughby Road. Daughter of H.H. Trapnell, and of Clara Trapnell. 13 March 1941, at 2 Willoughby Road.

TRAPNELL, HILDA MAY, age 27; of 2 Willoughby Road. Daughter of H.H. Trapnell, and of Clara Trapnell. 13 March 1941, at 2 Willoughby Road.

TRAVIS, AGNES, age 51; of 9 Erskine Rd. Wife of Percy Owen Travis. 12 March 1941 at 9 Erskine Rd

TRAVIS, PERCY OWEN, age 48; of 9 Erskine Road. Husband of Agnes Travis. 12 March 1941, at 9 Erskine Road.

TUFFLEY, VICTOR FIFIELD, age 18. Son of Mr. G. E. Tuffley, of 70 Norwood Road. 12 March 1941, at Lancaster Avenue.

TURNER, FLORENCE ELIZABETH, age 59; of 2 Pleasant Street. Daughter of the late Robert and Elizabeth Jane Davies; wife of Robert Thomas Turner. 21 December 1940, at 2 Pleasant Street.

TURNER, ROBERT THOMAS, age 59; of Pleasant Street. Son of the late Edward and Eleanor Turner; husband of Florence Elizabeth Turner. 21 December 1940. at 2 Pleasant Street.

TURNEY, FLORENCE, age 65; of 23 Church Street, Egremont. Wife of Samuel Turney. 12 March 1941, at 23 Church Street.

TYERS, WILLIAM OLIVER, age 69; of 54 Manor Road. 20 December 1940, at 54 Manor Road.

WALKER, ELIZABETH, age 28; of 4 Heathbank Avenue. Daughter of Margaret Hopkins, and of William Hopkins; wife of James Browel Walker. 21 December 1940 at 4 Heathbank Avenue.

WALKER, JAMES BROWEL, age 28; of 4 Heathbank Avenue. Husband of Elizabeth Walker. 21 December 1940, at 4 Heathbank Avenue.

WALLACE, ANNIE ELIZABETH, age 66; of 66 Serpentine Road. Wife of James Wallace. 21 December 1940, at 66 Serpentine Road.

WALLACE, JAMES, age 57; of 66 Serpentine Road. Husband of Annie Elizabeth Wallace. 21 December 1940, at 66 Serpentine Road.

WALLACE, WILLIAM, age 63; Special Constable; of 23 Elgin Drive. 20 December 1940, at 23 Elgin Dr.

WEARE, SYBIL MILDRED, age 55; of 6 Loretto Road. Daughter of the late Mr. and Mrs. Cottier, of Tintern Street, Walton, Liverpool; wife of Robert Weare. 12 March 1941, at 6 Loretto Road.

WEBSTER, EMILY FRANCIS of 85 Wallasey Village. Wife of Edward Webster. Injured 12 March 1941 at 83 Wallasey Village, died 15 March 1941 at Upton-by-Chester Hospital.

WEBSTER, SARAH, age 60; of 22 School Lane. 12 March 1941, at School Lane.

WESTCOTT, MARY ANN, age 75; of Manor Lodge, Manor Road. Daughter of the late Joshua and Frances McElroy; widow of Alfred John Westcott. 21 December 1940, at Manor Lodge.

WHITEHOUSE, FRANK, age 42; M.A.; Air Raid Warden. Son of Joseph Whitehouse, of 22 Kensington Road, Selly Park, Birmingham, and of the late Emma Whitehouse; husband of Barbara Mary Whitehouse, of 9 Leyburn Road. 12 March 1941, at Claremount Road.

WHITEHOUSE, JAMES, age 80; of 18 Carnsdale Road. Moreton. 20 Dec. 1940, at 18 Carnsdale Rd.

WHITTINGTON, ROBERT HENRY SAWER, age 67; of 2 Church Street, Egremont. Husband of the late Beatrice E. Whittington. 12 March 1941, at Church Street.

WILLAN, CHARLES HENRY, age 43; Home Guard; Firewatcher; of 25 Erskine Road. Son of Ada Willan, of 15 Lycett Road, and of the late John Charles Willan; husband of Hilda Willan. 12 March 1941, at 25 Erskine Road.

WILLIAMS, EVAN, age 59; A.R.P. Rescue Service; of 3 Ethel Terrace, Greasby, Upton, Wirral. Son of the late Mr. and Mrs. Thomas Williams. Injured 12 March 1941. at Poulton Road: died 14 March 1941, at Cottage Hospital.

WILSON, ELIZABETH ELLEN, age 53 of 70 Northbrook Road. Wife of Samuel Murray Wilson. 12 March 1941, at 68 Northbrook Road.

WILSON, MILDRED, age 42; of 26 Dovedale Road. Daughter of Isaac Newton. 20 December 1940, at 26 Dovedale Road.

WILSON, SAMUEL MURRAY, age 56; of 70 Northbrook Road. Husband of Elizabeth Ellen Wilson. 12 March 1941, at 68 Northbrook Road.

WINTERS, ALEXANDER MACUTCHEON, age 52; of 15 Foxhey Road. 12 March 1941, at 15 Foxhey Road.

WOODCOCK, WILLIAM HENRY, age 51; Home Guard; of 10 Foxhey Road. Husband of. Florence Woodcock. 12 March 1941, at 10 Foxhey Road.

WRIGHT, ALBERT ERNEST, age 54; of 8 Brockley Avenue, New Brighton. Husband of Sarah Elizabeth Wright. Injured 21 December 1940, at 8 Brockley Avenue; died same day at Leasowe Hospital.

YATES, JAMES, age 68. Husband of Mary Ellen Yates, of 2 Beaufort Square, Birkenhead. 12 March 1941, at City Line Sheds, Dock Road.

WARTIME REMINISCENCES

The following articles recall the experiences of people who lived through the war in Wallasey

Wallasey – Frontline Town

The impressions I received during the Second World War were many and various, and as a young teenager life was fill of expectancy as to what the morrow was going to bring. The plan of the civil defence proved itself a staunch bulwark of British resistance to air-attack. Air Raid Precautions (ARP) was roughly outlined in 1935, but was taken seriously after the 1938 September crisis. As soon as war threatened, Air Raid Wardens and special police went on duty; auxiliary firemen reported to their stations; the decontamination centres were ready in the event of a gas attack, and the hospitals were cleared to receive casualties. It was at this time that the people of Wallasey were supplied with those grotesque gas masks, which, when you put them on and breathed out, the rubber on the side of your face would start flapping, making an embarrassingly rude noise, often resulting in a fit of the giggles.

Outside ARP Wardens Posts, there were short poles or a staff, which had a square piece of plywood lying flat on it, and this would be painted a lime green colour. It was supposed to change colour should there be gas attack. That was the reason why everybody had to carry their gas-masks around with them for fear of a gas attack by the Germans.

Trenches were dug, shelters made, sandbags piled up, lights obscured; in fact the whole face of Britain was changed overnight. In the Parks, workmen were digging Air-Raid Shelters and as a school boy I learned quite a lot about how to dig a trench, how to join wood into making wall supports or roofing and how to make use of every available piece of land. We boys learnt quite a lot in those days before the War. Gradually sand bags made their appearance, as did Anderson Air-Raid Shelters, and of course later on 'the Morrison Table Shelters.

Anderson Air Raid Shelters were those weird contraptions which were made of corrugated steel parts and fitted together and placed in a hole in your garden, the excess soil being spread over the top of the shelters so as to form an extra cover. Morrison Table Shelters were instituted by the Rt Hon Herbert Morrison MP who was the Home Secretary from 1940 to 1945. These shelters were made of steel angles and sheets and when fitted together would form a table which could be used in the kitchen.

Between then and September 1939 many changes in Wallasey started to take place, the biggest being the establishment of the Barrage Balloons throughout the Borough. These Balloons were voluminous creatures, like gigantic silvery birds which were tethered to a steel hawser and allowed to ascend into the heavens, so as to protect the people living below in the town. A sky full of Balloons was a majestic and comforting sight, for they forced enemy aircraft to fly above them thereby making their targets harder to pin point. They were disbanded in 1945, at the end of the war.

Another reassuring sight was to see the 4.5 inch heavy ack-ack guns in their emplacements along Kings Parade and also behind the sandhills along Moreton foreshore. In addition to these guns, we had a rocket battery consisting of 64 single 'Z' projector rocket guns which were situated on the grounds of what is now the Warren Golf Club. This battery was eventually taken over by the 103rd Cheshire Home Guard so as to release the regular soldiers for more urgent duties overseas [see picture Below].

War Savings Campaigns which were started late in 1939, were becoming very popular and it was a way to stimulate our National War effort. Campaigns such as Warships Week or Airforce Week, were used to raise money for the services mentioned.

A 20 barrel, No 6, Mark One Projector Rocket being fired from the Waliasey 'Z' or Rocket Battery which was situated near the Bridge at the bottom of Sandcliffe Road (seen on the left). This was only one of six sites in the country to have this advanced rocket system which was installed by June 1944, replacing the single 'Z' Projector rocket guns. The Home Guard had taken over from the 104th Cheshires in early 1942. Air raid shelters can be seen either side of the rockets

According to the size of the town you would be allocated a target of say £300,000 which would help to adopt a ship in the Navy or to buy Fighters and Bombers for the Royal Air Force. This idea of saving really caught the imagination of the general public and according to statistics in 1200 savings areas over £400 million was saved.

Ration Books and Identity Cards were issued to everybody and the Post Office issued 6d Savings Stamps which were blue in colour with the Union Jack flying from a flag pole, which had a burning cross fixed to the top of the pole. I think the 2/6d stamps were similar but coloured red.

White lines began to appear on lamp posts, tree trunks and also curbs so you wouldn't hurt yourself in the Black-out. Everybody carried small torches with them, many had bits of brown paper covering the light, so as to keep the brilliance down.

In the early days Corporation Buses had all their windows painted blue with lighting kept low. People also got busy buying strips of gummed paper to decorate the windows of their homes. This was to ensure that flying glass was kept down to a minimum. Everybody knew War was imminent and we were just waiting for the word to be given, but first all the children had to be evacuated and this was a tremendous task which was carried out like a true military operation. My brother and I were evacuated to Newtown in . We were billeted there for eight months, but finally came home because nothing was happening. This period was known as the "Phoney War".

We were so full of confidence that nothing would ever harm us because we had the biggest Navy in the world, a magnificent Air Force and an Army second to none. What could possibly happen?

What indeed! War was declared on Sunday 3 September 1939 and on the 17 September the Aircraft Carrier Courageous was torpedoed and sunk. Insult to injury was added on 14 October 1939 when the Germans had the audacity to sail into Scapa Flow (which is situated in the Orkney Islands and is a UK Naval base) torpedoed and sank the Battleship Royal Oak with a great loss of life.

That was the beginning. By December of that year the Royal Navy had got some of its own back by forcing the German Pocket Battleship Admiral Graf Spee to scuttle itself outside Montevideo harbour on the 17 December. On the 16 February 1940 the Destroyer Cossack rescued over 300 British Seamen from the German supply/prison ship Altmark. By the following May to June, we had the evacuation of Dunkirk and on the 21 June 1940 France capitulated, thus leaving the way open for Hitler's grand offensive against England.

Things were beginning to look very bleak for us on this island fortress of ours.

The all conquering German Luftwaffe came in their hundreds to annihilate us and bomb us into submission, but it was in their hundreds that they were shot down and defeated by those gallant boys of the Royal Air Force. The Germans realised that the day time bombing of England was not their forte, so they switched to night time bombing and this is really where my story begins. The bombing of Wallasey started on the Saturday night of 10 August 1940. We had many blitz and raids until the culmination of them on the 10 December 1942 which was the date when the last bomb fell on Merseyside.

During these Air-Raids, many of the essential services, i.e., gas, water and electricity, were hit. Candles were always in great demand, but when a water wagon appeared on the streets, there was always a rush of people to replenish their stocks. I used to cycle around the roads with a bucket on my handle bars, and if I spotted a water wagon I would fill up my bucket and cycle home as quickly as possible and tell our neighbours where the wagon could be found. Notices were posted everywhere telling people to boil water, this was essential if you wanted to stay healthy.

The vast majority of the population had been motivated by the Air-Raids and many people, like ourselves, had a stirrup pump, a bucket of water and a bucket of sand or in some cases sandbags, at the ready to deal with any fires which might occur. Also people could go out shopping, having left their front door open, knowing full well that nobody would enter their house while they were away. Comradeship and trust were absolute, neighbours looked after and cared for each other.

During the height of the Air-Raids the Corporation would utilise the bombed areas for installing huge iron tanks for storing water to fight fires. These were known as EWS tanks (Emergency Water Supplies). There were also cast iron water pipes which stretched the whole length of roads with outlets at designated intervals which where also used for the same purpose, namely to fight fires.

Another innovation used by the Army was a queer contraption which had a barrel shaped chimney with a cowl on top and a burning box or furnace behind the chimney which burned oil. These vehicles were stationed at intervals along the main roads running parallel with the river. The idea being that when they received the Yellow Alert (ie. a warning that the enemy aircraft were approaching) the army would light these furnaces so as to make a smoke screen and thereby conceal the river and so fool the Enemy. This practice was all right if the wind was blowing from west to east but I am afraid that this didn't happen very often and they were eventually withdrawn.

I also remember the concrete Block Houses that were built along the main roads such as Seabank Road, Penkett Road and Warren Drive, which led to or from the Promenade, and of the concrete road blocks which were zealously guarded by the Home Guard.

Many a time at night, if you were travelling by bus to

The bomb crater on New Brighton Promenade following a raid on 1/2 May. Note the barage balloon above the baths

the cinema or the ferry, you would be stopped at these blocks and asked to produce your Identity Card and in some cases your gas mask.

On the slipways leading to the shore from the Promenade there would be concrete pyramid blocks the purpose of which was to stop enemy tanks from coming ashore. The Promenade itself was full of these concrete obstacles which looked very impressive.

Further along the Promenade, past Derby Bathing Pool, you would come across Leasowe Golf Club and also the surrounding sandhills. This area was all mined in case of invasion, but unfortunately the only lives it claimed were those of four boys of similar age to myself. They were Peter Dennis Burkes aged 12, Desmond Caunce Robinson aged 13 and John Fergus Smith aged 10 all killed on the 13 March 1941 on the minefield at Leasowe Golf Club. The other boy John Murphy aged 10 was killed on 13 April 1941 on Leasowe Sandhills.

One of my hobbies during the War was to collect Shrapnel and the bigger the pieces you had the more the other lads would look up to you. All schools were closed after an Air-Raid, and after one in particular, my friend and I went down on our bicycles to the Promenade to see what we could collect. This would be about 5am on 2 May 1941. It had been rather a heavy raid and unknown to us this was the start of the May Blitz. As we cycled along the Promenade towards Derby Bathing Pool, we came across a neat hole in the road and as we got off our bikes to have a better look we saw the tail fin of a bomb. It was nice and shiny so we decided that we would have another look at it when we came back from the baths; but we never got the chance. By then the Police had arrived and had roped the area off and of course we were told to clear off with a flea in our ear. That bomb exploded about 6 hours later making a huge crater.

A few days later again in the same area I saw lots of boys on the shore picking up Incendiary Bombs. These devices where highly inflammable and could kill if not handled with the utmost care. It would appear, so the

story goes, that a German Bomber was shot down, but before ditching it dropped a "bread basket" of Incendiaries. These having partly been burned out in the water or having been well and truly soaked were now being collected.

Not to be outdone I also went onto the shore and collected thirteen bombs myself. When I got back onto the Promenade I noticed that these lads were banging the bombs on the sea wall to loosen the cap which is situated on the base of the bomb. Once this was loosened you could unscrew it and shake the damp phosphorous out thereby make the bomb safe. If, however, your found a brown metal cap inside the casing, you would ditch it immediately as this was a second and highly active fuse liable to explode at any moment. A few of these were found by the lads who discarded them right away. I took the belt of my mackintosh and fed it through the fins of the bombs, all thirteen of them and took them home feeling very pleased with myself. Having placed them in the back garden I called my mother and asked her to come and see what I had got. I will leave it to your imagination as to what she said. Incidently the belt to my mack was ruined. No need for me to tell you how mad we were in those days but all lads were like that. This was a war time adventure on the Home Front and we were thoroughly enjoying ourselves.

One early morning during the May Blitz when all had gone quiet and it was still dark, we noticed that there appeared to be a large red glow over Liverpool. As we lived close to the river my mother took my brother and myself down Dalmorton Road to the river front. The sight that met our eyes was truly unbelievable. The whole of the Liverpool waterfront from Seaforth right down to Dingle, a distance of 7 to 8 miles, was one solid mass of flame and most amazing of all could be seen the silhouettes of the Royal Liver Building, the Cunard Building and the Mersey Docks and Harbour Board all standing like sentinels. It was a sight that I shall never forget. The Germans really gave us a hammering during this May Blitz and they must have gone back to their base in occupied Europe thinking that they had finally knocked out the Port of Liverpool. The cinemas of Wallasey were a great place to go for relaxation but there were times when a notice would appear on the screen which would inform you that there was an "Air-Raid in progress. You are advised to take shelter". Not many people left because in theory, the reckoning was that you could quite as easily be killed going home, as you could by sitting in the cinema. Posters had a heyday during the War years urging you to be ever vigilant. "Save Fuel to make munitions for Battle". "Beat Firebomb Fritz, Britain shall not burn." "Dig for Victory." "Keep Mum - she's not so dumb." "Careless talk cost lives." "They talked – this happened" but the one I remember best goes like this:-

When you've news of our Munitions. Keep it Dark.
Ships or planes or troop positions. Keep it Dark.
Lives are lost through conversation
Here's a tip for the Duration
When you've news or information. Keep it Dark.

The Home Front

Do you remember the BBC Home Service and the Light Programme; here is the news and this is Alvar Liddell or Stuart Hibbert reading it; John Snagge reporting from the Front; the old favourite "Germany Calling" by Lord Haw Haw and the Kitchen Front with Frederick Grisewood and Mabel Constanduros; the Radio Doctor, Music while you work and Workers Playtime; ITMA (Its That Man Again) with Tommy Handley. "Hello Playmates" with Arthur Askey, "Much Binding in the Marsh" with Kenneth Horne and Stinker Murdoch and "Hi Gang" with Bebe Daniels and Ben Lyon and many more. It was programmes like these which kept us in high spirits during those dark days.

Food Rationing

And what about food rationing in mid War? Here is an example of a typical weeks ration:- 2oz of tea, 8oz sugar, 4oz jam, 2oz lard, 2oz butter, 2oz margarine, 1oz cheese, 4oz bacon, 3/4lb of meat and one egg, if you were lucky. The meat could be supplemented with corned beef. Potatoes 5lb for 6d, a small loaf would cost 2 3/4d [1p] and a large loaf 41/2d [2p] (all off white) and milk 2 1/2d pint [1 p]. About 3 pints of milk a week were allowed. There were two particular pages in your ration book which were marked Personal Points (sweets) and these pages were subdivided into columns marked D and E. There were 4Ds marked D1 and 4 Es marked El, thereby indicating that these were four weeks in the first month. Likewise when month 2 arrived the D and E coupons would be marked D2 and E2 and so on to the end of the year. At the height of the rationing you could get 3ozs of sweets or chocolate, usually Cadbury's Blended, from your coupons per week. One ounce for D and two ounces for E.

Even in those days you could have a good meal from the British Restaurant and quite tasty too I might say. A typical menu would be roast beef, roast potatoes, peas, gooseberry tart and custard and a cup of tea all for 9d [4p]. Two British Restaurants which I used to frequent were situated above the Palace Fair Ground, New Brighton and on the first floor above Woolworths, Grange Road, Birkenhead.

Babies and young children would have bottles of cod liver oil and orange juice free. Infant children, expectant mothers and invalids would have more milk. Food rationing started in January 1940 and clothing was rationed from June 1941.

Cigarettes were scarce during and after the War and they were either sold loose or in paper wrappers with the particular brand printed on them. This was one way of saving paper for the War effort. Special buckets were also issued to keep your potato peelings in and also all discarded vegetables and such like. These were collected every other day for the farmers so as they could use it for pig swill.

USA

Life started to look up a bit when the Yanks came over here. They brought spam and gum, lots of it and of course not forgetting the Jitterbug. They also brought some sunshine into our lives and at last we weren't alone. "Any Gum Chum" and "Mr Chad - What No?" were sayings which originated with the arrival of the US Armed Forces. The more the Germans bombed us the more we became united. If the men in the Armed Forces could grin and bear it, so could we - especially an excitable and at times a fool hardy young teenager (weren't we all).

B A Thomson

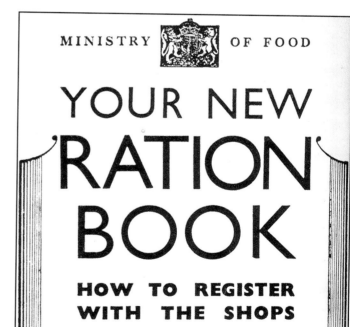

MINISTRY ✠ OF FOOD

YOUR NEW 'RATION' BOOK

HOW TO REGISTER WITH THE SHOPS

The new Ration Books are now being distributed. As soon as you receive your new Book you must fill in the particulars as explained below, and then take the Book to the shops for fresh Registration. It has been found possible to allow *immediate* Registration, and the sooner you register the better.

The Wallasey Blitz 1940–1941

When I was born, the Second World War was still fresh in the memories of everybody: who had endured it. I was brought up in a house in Bowden Road off Belvidere Road – which had been rebuilt in 1951 as a replacement for one damaged in the "Wallasey Blitz". I listened to my Grandmother who had lost her home in Wheatland Lane Seacombe, albeit that she was living in Cambridge at the time, my Grandfather having been moved there following the bombing of Paul's Flour Mill on the Dock Road Wallasey where he had worked. I came to believe that Poulton and Seacombe had been virtually wiped out as the Germans endeavoured to destroy the docks and the other areas of Wallasey where more well to do persons lived had with minor exceptions been spared the worst of the damage, but like most other facts about the Second World War, as I originally learnt them, the truth was somewhat different.

1940.

Despite the war starting in September 1939 Wallasey did not experience any bombing until August 1940. This in itself is interesting, insofar that it corresponds with the commencement of the Battle of Britain. During the course of the year 1940 Wallasey was to experience officially eighteen air raids, but this is misleading because several raids are listed in the official reports as lasting up to three days, this is particularly the case for the incidents that occurred in December 1940 and in March 1941. The December attacks took place over three nights, 20th to 23rd with the heaviest night being the second. Various types of bombs were employed, incendiary, high explosive, semi armour piercing and parachute mines. Damage was scattered across the whole of the borough but the worst incidents occurred at Brockley Avenue, Dalmorton Road, Sandrock Road, Earlston Road, Manor Road, Withens Lane, Croxteth Avenue, Chepstow Avenue, Serpentine Road, Poulton Road, Clifford Road and Carnsdale Road Moreton. There were a 121 deaths and 258 persons injured. This was by far the worst the town had so far experienced and whilst the number of locations appears limited it must be observed that blast damage and disturbance to structures and people occurred on a much wider basis leaving few people untouched, even Victoria Central Hospital had to be evacuated. Of personal interest it was in this raid that a terrace of houses in Sandrock Road was hit, very badly damaged and subsequently had to be demolished. It was upon the foundations of these properties that my house was built. Still visible on surrounding houses are the shrapnel marks and the marks of modifications and repairs which resulted from the damage. Two people were killed in the Sandrock Road bombing, Mrs. Muriel Badham, age 47 and Edith Agnes Bellas age 65.

1941

The New Year of 1941 saw a brief raid on the morning of the 2nd January [05.04 to 06.04hrs], damage was done to the Mariners Homes.

Seven days later on the 9th January the twentieth raid on Wallasey resulted in high explosive bombs damaging Sandringham Drive, Pennine Road and Albion Street. At this point there was a lull in the German offensive because of the winter weather. Bombing was very restricted over the whole country and it was March before Wallasey saw its next raid and most sustained and damaging attacks, on consecutive nights of the 12th, 13th, and 14th. Extensive destruction was wrought on Seacombe, Poulton, Liscard, Wallasey village, and New Brighton. In all 174 people were killed and 158 injured. Again Victoria Central Hospital was evacuated despite the fact that it was accommodating over a 100 casualties at the time, and had been protected by an estimated 90,000 sandbags. The Wallasey Fire Brigade, which was now part of the National Service, had to employ 450 men and 60 pumps and appliances. It is estimated that over this period 316 aircraft from two German air fleets, Luftflotte II and Luftflotte III attacked the Mersey area, dropping 303 tonnes of bombs. By way of comparison Birkenhead suffered 264 people killed, and 40 people where killed in Liverpool.

Again on a personal note the house 13 Bowden Road had received a direct hit destroying it and causing the adjoining semi detached house (No. II) to be badly damaged, the rebuilt 11 Bowden Road where I was born was to be my home for 30 years. Two people died in No. 13 - Margaret Sawyer age 79 and her 16 year old grandson Robert H. Speakman. In the house in Halton Road backing onto the damage Mr. and Mrs. Alred were temporarily made homeless, soon they were to suffer further tragedy when their only son, Gunner Alred, was killed in action in the Western Desert during the summer of 1941.

In total 320 people were killed in Wallasey; there were 509 alerts, 1,044 separate incidents and 700 high explosive bombs landed In the Borough. On a national basis these are fractional statistics. By way of comparison, during the war 29,890 people were killed in the London area alone, whilst 30,705 were killed elsewhere in the country and considerable damage was done to German towns by Allied bombing. But at the time, and to all who suffered, the experience was traumatic and unique.

Peter O'Brien

The remains of a car can be seen in the right hand driveway of a bomb-damaged house in Claremount Road. Wallasey Cricket Club ground is in the background

Mill Lane Hospital

The present day Victoria Central Hospital in Mill Lane was originally built as an Isolation Hospital for infectious diseases, mainly Diphtheria and Scarlet Fever, with a sanatorium and chest clinic for Tuberculosis cases. These diseases were most prevalent throughout pre-war years and the hospital was very busy.

During the War there was also an isolation block for soldiers from nearby units who had developed diseases such as Measles, Mumps and Typhoid who needed to be nursed in quarantine to prevent spread of infection.

On May 6th 1941 Ward 2, in the grounds of Mill Lane Hospital, received a direct hit during a bombing raid. This was the male Diphtheria Ward and very sadly two children were killed, namely John Byrne and John Bellamy. The Night Nurse, Mary Randles (now Carlisle), was alone on duty at the time but another nurse, Sister Ruth Beattie, really on day duty, returned immediately to help her with the patients.

Near the main entrance from Mill Lane a land mine had descended into a tree and hung dangling from the parachute cords. Because of this threat the whole hospital had to be evacuated via the already bombed houses in Leominster Road. Nurses returning for duty at the hospital helped with the evacuation of the patients and these included Nurse Peggy Jones (later Pemberton), Joe Pemberton also Billy McKillop and John Hampson both porters. Father McNally, the priest from St. Alban's Church, nearby, helped Nurse Randles to check that all the wards were free of occupants.

All the patients, including soldiers from "Darley Dene", the house in Breck Road, were moved firstly to the air raid shelters within the grounds and thence to Egerton Grove School. Sister Trees, a Sister Tutor, Nurse Walker, and Nurse Randles made the final check in the hospital for personnel and patients, collected drugs and equipment from the Theatre and walked to Egerton Grove School. They presented quite a sight in their crumpled dirty uniforms and faces blackened from the debris of the blitz.

Standing outside Ward 2 Mill Lane Fever Hospital are: left, an Irish Ward Maid, Sister Ruth Beatty and Peggy (Jones) Pemberton. Note the sandbags on the left and roof damage

Mary Carlisle (nee Randles) is photographed at Mill Lane Hospital. Ward 4 is on the left and Ward 1 is on the right with an air raid shelter

On arrival at the school patients were bedded down an the floors for the remainder of the night, with food and drink being provided by the Wallasey Fire Service and Air Raid personnel with makeshift canteen facilities being set up in the playground. As soon as it was daylight the seriously ill patients were all sent to the hospital at Clatterbridge accompanied by nurse Mary Randles and Peggy Jones, and there they remained for three months before returning to Mill Lane.

Peggy Pemberton and Mary Carlisle

[Peggy Jones and Joe Pemberton were married in April 1947 and are still living in Wallasey 53 years later to tell this story.]

I Remember I Remember. ....

..... as a member of the Wallasey Silver Band being joined at our rehearsals held in a large wooden hut in Wallasey Village, by some soldiers from the Pioneer Corps. Prior to "call-up" they had been members of the famous Black Dyke Mills band. I remember hearing the tragic news that their billet at "Darley Dene" in Breck Road, had received a direct hit and that they had all been killed.

.. .... being rejected on medical grounds for the RAF; joining the Home Guard and being based at St Nicholas Church. Those without rifles were given broom handles for parades and a little tin filled with pebbles, the significance of which did not manifest itself until we had an exercise which involved the territorials acting as the enemy. The manoeuvres took place in the sandhills at Harrison Drive and we were to surprise the so called "Germans" by rattling our tins, the sound of which was supposed to represent machine gun fire, and take them prisoner.

..... standing outside our local community shelter at the bottom of Ilford Avenue, looking up at a German bomber then witnessing the flash and bang of the explosion of the bomb as the Ritz Cinema in Birkenhead received its direct hit.

Jack Stevenson

The Film Now Showing . . . . . .

What, to my knowledge, was one of the first bombing raids on Merseyside, hit my favourite toy shop in Rake Lane, Wallasey. Within a few weeks they'd reopened again in a vacant shop premises just around the corner in Magazine Lane, with a complete new stock of toys that were still in plentiful supply at that time. In the meantime they claimed war damage from the government and had their former shop completely restored, moving back there within six months. But believe it or not, in less than a year later a second German bomb demolished their shop again but this time the government wouldn't pay war damage for the same site. To this day the site remains vacant, occupied only by a large advertising hoarding.

As we came into summer 1940 everyone on Merseyside was getting used to nightly raids by the Luftwaffe, and on one occasion a bomb aimed at New Brighton railway station missed and hit the rear of my local cinema only yards away. Fortunately, it only badly damaged an old house at the rear of the Winter Gardens that was originally used as dressing rooms for the old theatre that had formerly occupied the site. In later years I spoke with the chief projectionist who was on duty the Saturday night when the bomb fell. At that moment he was looking out through the projection room ports at the screen, when suddenly there was a loud bang and the screen seemed to jump out from the stage towards him. Of course the Winter Gardens was built as a theatre and had a large stage, the screen being suspended from the flies above the stage in order that it could be flown upwards when they had a stage presentation. The blast from the bomb blew it outwards, but It Immediately fell back to it's original position without suffering any damage. However, it appears that the film due to be shown the following week must have been in those old dressing rooms, because when I went there on the Monday evening, over the nicely printed poster advertising the current film attraction, was a hand written notice saying that "owing to enemy action there was a change in programme - the film now showing was "Naughty Marietta" starring Nelson Eddy and Jeanette MacDonald.

Clive Garner

Rear view of the Coliseum Cinema, Wallasey Village which was destroyed by fire on the night of 13/14 March 1941

A Teenager's View of Wallasey at War

I was 16 when the Second World War commenced and my father, Luke, became a Special Constable. I joined the A.R.P. Wardens as a messenger riding my pedal cycle from A.R.P. Post to A.R.P. Post usually during a bombing raid when they started. I was stationed at St. Pauls Road Recreation Ground, then in the basement of the Concert Hall in Manor Road and then in the post in Church Street. After about 18 months I volunteered for the National Fire Service Observer Section. Only one in two volunteers were selected for this section as the fatality rate was high due to the hazardous nature of the job. I was usually stationed on top of the flour silos on the docks - the only snag being if the building was hit the only way down was either a 200 feet dive into the dock or into the cobbled courtyard below. Going back to the A.R.P. time I was very naive. One night I was told by a lady that there was an unexploded incendiary bomb in her garden. I put it on a shovel and carried it into the A.R.P. Post and placed it on the table and asked what I should do with it. I have never seen Wardens move so fast and I was told in uncomplimentary terms what to do with it. Whilst I was with the A.R.P. a bomb fell on the post in St Pauls Road and they were all killed. Later on - whilst the bombing was still in progress (about 1942) I was attached to the sub-fire station in Rullerton Road (where the garage is now situated). There was just the one fire engine stationed there. One evening it went to a fire in Breck Road. I remember there was farm land there and unfortunately one of the firemen inadvertently fell into the cesspit. His colleagues would not let him into the cab for the return journey which he had to make perched on the back of the fire engine. On arrival at Rullerton Road he had to stand in the Fire Station yard in the nude whilst I hosed him down! One very sad occasion was when my father's best friend, also a special constable, was putting up warning notices around an unexploded land mine in (I think) the Erskine Road area when it exploded and he was killed. The Special Constables usually worked in pairs and quite often would come across a suicide who would have hung themselves over the crater of what had been there house in which their family had been killed. The inexperienced constable would be told to get hold of the legs whilst his colleague cut the rope. Of course the inevitable happened and the dead weight would knock the Junior officer into the crater - I always felt that this showed a sick mentality but thankfully the majority of Constables were decent blokes.
At the end of the War I joined the Royal Observer Corps and served with them for over 40 years.

Sydney Pope (as related to Ray Lewis).

WARDEN POST 9A, St. Georges Road School
This photograph was taken in the Boys' Yard of the school after the uniforms had arrived. Previously the Wardens had worn armbands. **Front Row:** L/R No.3 Mr Yourston, No.4 Mr Jones, No.6 Mr Fetherick, 7 Jack Webster.
Second Row: No.I Dorothy Jones, No.2 Ephraim Jones, No.3 Mr Callum, No.5 Mr. Webb, No.6 Florrie Whitfield, No.9 Mrs Schofield.
Third Row No.2 Miss Garden, No.3 Roy Slack, No.4 Peggy Collins, No.5 Mr Stanley.

ARP Wardens Post 9A met in the cellar at St Georges Rd School, Wallasey Village. The cellar was also used as an air raid shelter by the pupils during the daytime, which is where most of them learnt their multiplication tables. Five wardens of Group 9 lost their lives in the Blitz of March 1941.

Shirley Abbott

Harry Reid

Harry was nearly 14 at the start of the war, and a pupil at Oldershaw Grammar school. He was a member of the Air Training Corps, who met at the "Navy League" in Withens Lane.

When the air raids started he also joined the Auxiliary Fire service as a messenger, the chief requirement being access to a bicycle. As soon as the air raid siren sounded the messengers reported to the fire station in Manor Road and awaited orders.

A lasting memory for all who were in Wallasey during the March blitz, was the presence of numerous fire appliances from small Lancashire towns with their crews, who had come to give some relief to our stretched emergency services. Every street in the vicinity of Liscard had vehicles parked in them. Harry told of meeting a close friend holding the hand of his small sister and looking rather lost in Liscard and on chatting to him, he was told that their Mother had been killed the night before along with their brother's fiancee.

After one of the raids, Harry was tipped off that a large quantity of incendiary bombs had fallen on the beach at Harrison Drive, so he went off on his trusted bike and hung as many as possible on the bike and sold these as souvenirs to the out of town firemen. It is said that he opened his first bank account with the proceeds.

Barbara Reid

Home Guard Rocket Battery

Early in 1942 I joined the 104/103 "Z" AA Home Guard Rocket Battery, it was situated on the Warren Golf Course on Sea Road, Wallasey. Being amongst the first volunteers, I was trained by the regular RA officers and NCO's on the quite primitive single projectors. On passing out training I fired this anti-aircraft weapon at Freshfield, near Formby, over the water from Wallasey. It was raining heavily as the hundred or so men marched from James Street station behind the Liver Buildings to board the Formby train from the Exchange station. Tin hats and capes were worn; all of us must have looked like a draft of soldiers marching to the docks to embark overseas. Many of us were kissed "Good Bye" by the "Black Shawl" old Liverpool women. God bless them, they weren't to know we wore home guard flashes under our capes and that we would all be in our own beds that night.

What an experience the practice shoot turned out to be for a 15 year old lad, yes I had added two years on top of my real age to be accepted into the new HGAA unit. I was known as "Young Mac" throughout my service with the HG After this training shoot, everyone found the back of their boots blistered and the pile of our trousers singed off, by the flaming rear of the rocket shells.

Having passed our course on single projectors I stayed in A I troop which now manned twin projectors. Every fourth night was training and every eighth was all night duty, billets were in Danehurst Road. An evening meal was provided and plenty of it, the sweet was always prunes, prunes, prunes. Breakfast was porridge, eggs and bacon. Many of the lads took doggy bags of bacon home to supplement their families rations.

Twice in 1943 the lull battery of 64 projectors fired a "fire power" demonstration, shooting off 128x3inch shells in one go. These exploded over a safe area above the Mersey. About two minutes later the sea boiled as tons of shrapnel fell from 10,000 feet. The ground dust took about three minutes to settle. The Cheshire County army badge was the cap badge worn. The red and black bow and arrow 4th area AA.

Command Square was the divisional sign and the red triangle efficiency badge was the arm insignia worn. On the eight-day rota manning system some 1,600 to 1,800 gunners were required to keep the battery operational. The commanding officer was Major Harley MBE MC. The photograph on page 46 taken from "Jockey Lane" (Sandcliffe Road) during Sunday Shoot shows a flight of rockets leaving twin projectors. The railway embankment forms part of the horizon.

Fred McEneany

Wharfedale Road Fire-fighting Group

At the request of my Uncle, Capt. HVB Thorpe, 2nd in Command "C" Company Home Guard, stationed at New Brighton Rugby Club, Reeds Lane, Leasowe, I organised a group of friends to form a rota for secretarial duties. One of these was Hazel Blackburn who left later to join the WAAF eventually being posted as a wireless operator at Western Approaches, Derby House, Liverpool. The evenings we were on duty we were called for by car and taken to the HQ's The journey was often very bumpy due to the potholes from bomb debris. We were often late getting home having to wait for air raids to cease and the "All Clear" sound.

Street Fire Fighting Groups were formed to combat the damage by incendiary bombs to people and property. We had a friendly group in Wharfedale Road and practised putting out Imaginary fires using stirrup pump, buckets for water and sand, sandbags, garden rakes, bin lids as shields and a rain-butt was kept In the passage-ways between our houses.

The members of our group were:- No.2 David & Madge Rogers; No.4 Chaddock family plus Cartwrights; No.6 Wilding Family; No.8 McLean Family; No.10 Len & Madge Makinson; No.12 Huntingtons.

We also kept ourselves cheerful mixing socially on quiet raid-free evenings, singing songs to David Roger's accompaniment. We even had one composed about us, words by T Arnold Chaddock (my father) and music by Len Makinson – a great worker for charity with his musical talents.

Joan T. Jones (nee Chaddock)

Wharfedale Road Fire-fighting Group
Top Row:- Mr McLean, his son, David Rogers, Michael Wilding, Mr Wilding, Mr T Arnold Chaddock
Second Row:- Mrs Huntington, Mrs Wilding, Mrs Jessie Cartwright Mrs Flo Chaddock, Joan Chaddock, Mrs McLean.
First Row:- Mrs Madge Rogers, Mrs Madge Makinson, Marguerite Chaddock Mr Huntington.
Front:- Mr Len Makinson.

INDEX

Gordon Rd. 15, 16
Gorsebank Rd. 15, 17
Gorsedale Rd. 24, 27
Gorsehill Rd. 24
Gorsey Lane 11,14,16, 18, 27
Great Float Hotel 12-13
Greaves B 36
Green CO 28
Green Lane 36
Greenwood La. 11, 16-17
Gregory BJ 40
Gregory Mrs E 40
Gregory JN 36
Griffin GA 28, 33
Griffiths Mrs AJM 40
Griffiths G 40
Griffiths R 36
Grisdale WW 10, 21, 40
Grosvenor Dr. 16, 24
Grosvenor Rd. 13, 24
Grosvenor St. 11, 27
Grove Rd. 27
Grove Rd. Station 35
Gutteridge Miss FM 26
Haig Ave. 16, 18
Halliday Ms E 40
Halton Rd. 24, 50
Hamilton Rd. 15, 16
Hampson Ms H 40
Hampson J 51
Hampstead Rd. 15, 17
Hanson CH 40
Hanson PD 40
Hardy Ave. 24
Harley TW 30, 54
Harrison Drive 13, 16, 18, 20, 23, 27, 36, 51, 53
Harrison F. 26
Harrison G 41
Harrison Hall 35
Harrison L 26
Harrison RH 28
Hartington Rd. 24
Harvey Rd. 15, 16
Hawarden Ave. 22
Hawkins E 26
Haws ER 9
Hawthorn Rd. 22
Hawthorne Gr. 12
Hay La. 16, 18
Hazeldene Ave. 13, 23
Heaney Mrs S 9
Heap AW 34
Heath F 36
Heath Bank 16, 18
Heaton C 25
Heaton Mrs EE 41
Henderson AF 36
Higgins P 41
Highet C 36
Hill WJ 36
Hillcroft Rd. 15, 17-18
Hillside Rd. 13, 15, 18
Hipkiss DH 41
Hogg R 28
Holden G 41
Holland Rd. 15, 16, 24
Holliday HB 34
Holroyd Mrs E 41
Holroyd Miss M 41
Hope St. 15

Hopkins W 41
Hounsome Ms BM 41
Howard C 41
Howard Mrs E 41
Howie J 35, 36
Hoylake Rd. 15, 18
Huck R 36
Hughes EH 41
Hughes Mrs FE 41
Hughes G 41
Hughes KS 41
Hughes LJ 41
Hughes M 41
Hughes Miss R 41
Hughes RB 41
Hughes W 28
Huntington A 41
Huntington J 41
Huntington Mr 54
Huntington Mrs 54
Hurst Miss JM 41
Huston W 41
Ilford Ave. 16, 18, 51
Imperial Ave. 16
Inger AR 26
Ingham H 36
Ingleby Rd. 11
Inglewood Rd. 24
Jack Miss G 41
Jack Miss L 41
Jack Mrs SM 41
Jackson Rev FC 28
James AC 41
Jardine WM 26
Jarrett WM 41
Jefferies J 26
Jefferson J 10, 41
Jennings Miss K 41
Jennings Miss LE 41
JenningsMiss M 41
Jennings Mrs S 41
Jennings W 41
Jervis Miss J 26
Joan Ave. 16, 18, 22
Johns Miss P 25
Johnston JH 41
Johnstone WP 28
Jones Ms A 41
Jones E 26
Jones Mrs EL 25, 26
Jones G 28
Jones GD 26
Jones Miss P 51
Jones PH 26
Jones Mrs MAF 26
Jones PL 41
Jones TAN 36
Joynson JR 36
Jupp AR 26
Karslake Rd. 22
Keir DF 26
Kelland Mrs AS 41
Kelly Miss CL 41
Kelvin Rd. 12, 15, 17 24
Kendrick Mrs FE 42
Kendrick TH 42
Kenilworth Rd. 15, 17
Kent Rd. 23
Kewley HS 25
King EC 26
Kingham H 26

Kings Pd. 23-24, 27, 46
King St. 27
Kingsley Rd. 15, 17
Kingsmead Rd. 12
Kingsway 16, 27
Kinnaird Rd. 15-16
Kirby J 26
Kirk Cottages 13
Knaresborough Rd. 15, 18
Knight EH 42
Knight Miss FM 42
Knight Mrs MW 42
Knox HJ 26
Laburnum Rd. 23
Ladeywood Rd. 15, 17
Lamont Mrs MM 42
Lancaster Ave. 21
Langdale Rd. 15-16
Larcombe FD 25-26
Latham Ms MA 42
Lauder AS 42
Laurie E 28
Lavell Mrs MA 42
Lawson JD 42
Lawton RM 42
Leander Rd. 23
Leary Miss EM 42
Leasowe Golf Club 35, 48
Leasowe Rd. 15, 36
Lee S 28
Leigh Mrs F 42
Leigh Miss PF 42
Leigh WE 36
Leominster Rd. 15, 17
Lewis Mrs FM 42
Lewis J 36
Lewis R 52
Leyburn Rd. 15,18
Leyne RW 26
Lickfold Mrs EF 42
Lilly Grove 11-12
Linden Gr. 13
Linwood Rd. 11
Liscard & Poulton R'way
Station 16, 18
Liscard Rd. 15,17
Litt C 36
Little Ms AH 42
Little Mrs E 42
Littledale Rd. 11
Little Hope St. 24
Lloyd Mrs H 9
Lockwood AG 36
Lofthouse SF 26
Lofthouse SJ 28
Longland Rd. 13
Low Mr. 22
Lumley Rd. 15,17
Lycett Rd. 20
Lymington Rd.15, 18, 27
Lyndhurst Rd. 24
Lythgoe JD 26
McAulay FJ 36
McDonald AA 26, 28
MacDonald ER 26
McDonald J 42
McEneany F 54
McGregor Mrs A 42
McGregor B 42
McGregor Miss E 42

McHarrie T 36
MckDunn J 26, 28
McKillop B 51
McKinley WD 36
McLean Mr 54
McLean Mrs 54
McMillan WB 28
McNally Ftr. 51
McNally Miss G 42
McQuone JJ 10
Machell HR 26
Maddock WW 42
Maddox CE 42
Magazine La. 16, 24, 27, 52
Mainwaring WT 42
Makinson L 54
Makinson Mrs M 54
Malvern Rd. 27
Manor La. 16, 24, 27
Manor Rd. 15, 17, 34, 36, 50, 52, 53
Mansfield JJ 34
Marlowe Rd. 27
Mariners Homes 50
Marks E 34
Maris Stella Cvt. 32
Marriott AS 42
Marriott Mrs J 42
Martin A 42
Martlew Mrs NE 42
Massey H 9
Massey Park 27
Mathieson F 26, 28
Matkinson L 54
Matkinson Mrs M 54
Maxfield JT 42
Meadowside 12
Meadway 27
Mealor H 42
Meldrum WP 25
Melling Rd. 15-16
Merton Rd. 13, 15, 18
Mickle L 35-36
Mill La. 11, 14, 16, 18, 21, 24
Mill La. Hosp. 51
Millet W 28
Millthwaite Rd. 15, 18
Mitchell J. 9
Molyneux Dr. 16, 27
Mollington Rd. 17
Monmouth Rd. 15, 18
Montgomery J 26, 28
Moore CL 42
Moore Mrs ME 42
Moore RS 36
Morrington Rd. 15
Morris HTK 36
Morris Miss RN 26
Morrison H 46
Moss CW 36
Moss FL 36
Mostyn St. 15, 18, 23
Mount The 24
Mount Rd. 15-16, 27
Mount Pleasant Road 11, 15-16
Munce Mrs HL 43
Munce TE 43
Murphy J 43, 48
Navy League 19, 53

Netherton Rd. 15, 19
New Brighton
    Cricket Club 21, 23
    Palace 49
    Railway Stn. 52
    Rugby Club 35, 54
    Tower 27, 31-33
Newall RV 36
Nield Mrs HM 43
Nield S 43
Noble Miss E 43
North Reserve 13
Noscoe Miss ME 43
Oakdale Ave. 23
Oakdale Rd. 24, 27
Oakley WC 36
Oddie HS 36
Offlands G 28
Oldershaw Sch. 27, 36, 53
Oldfield Mrs M 43
Oldfield W 43
Old Wallaseyans 35
Operation
    "Acorn" 35
    "Helen" 35
    "US" 35
Ormerod J 5, 35
Oxton Rd. 27
Owens SL 28
Pack WG 34
Palatine Rd. 11, 15, 17, 27, 32
Palermo St. 12
Palmeston Rd. 15, 18
Pappin Mrs E 43
Parfitt GL 26, 28, 33
Parker Mrs 43
Parker GN 28
Parker J 43
Parry St. 23
Parry Miss K 26
Parsons TH 36
Pasture Rd. 15, 18
Patterson RS 43
Paul's Mill 50
Pauls Rec. Ground 13
Peers Ms MA 43
Pemberton J 51
Pemberton Mrs P 51
Penkett Rd. 15-16, 35, 47
Penn V 25
Pennine Rd. 19, 50
Pennington PS 36
Pennington H 25, 28
Pennington Ald. J 36
Pennington Mrs KM 25,28
Petrie Mrs EA 43
Pickard AW 26
Pickering Rd. 15
Pickstock PE 26
Pollitt H 35, 36
Pope S 52
Portland St. 36
Potter F 28
Potter Mrs J 43
Poulton Rd. 14-15, 17-18, 27, 50
Pownall HJ 36
Preston W 43

BYE-BYE G
Be a Handwashing Superhero!

Dr. Katie Laird Prof. Sarah Younie Jules Marriner

BYE-BYE GERMS

Be a Handwashing Superhero!

By Katie Laird, Sarah Younie and Jules Marriner

with thanks to Sapphire Crosby

Published in 2020 by
Medina Publishing
50 High Street, Cowes, Isle of Wight, PO31 7RR
United Kingdom
Tel: +441983300044
info@medinapublishing.com

Paperback ISBN: 978-1-911487-48-7
eBook ISBN: 978-1-911487-47-0

Published in association with De Montfort University,
The Gateway, Leicester, LE1 9BH, UK
www.dmu.ac.uk

A catalogue record for this book is available from
The British Library

Bye-Bye Germs is part of A Germ's Journey series
www.germsjourney.com

Medina Publishing

DE MONTFORT
UNIVERSITY
LEICESTER

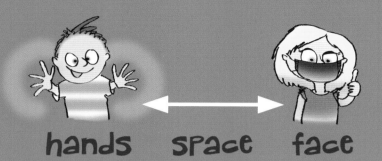

hands　space　face

This book belongs to

_____

BYE-BYE GERMS
Be a Handwashing Superhero!

Dr. Katie Laird   Prof. Sarah Younie   Jules Marriner

Medina Publishing

FOREWORD

Bye-By Germs: Be a Handwashing Superhero by microbiologist Dr Katie Laird and education specialist Professor Sarah Younie raises awareness and communicates the importance of handwashing at a young age.

"Because they cannot see germs, children often don't understand the need to wash their hands. Since the outbreak of COVID-19, we have all been told how important it is to wash our hands properly and regularly to prevent the virus spreading, but explaining to children the reasons why is equally as important.

"We have developed Bye-Bye Germs to teach young children about hand hygiene and help them identify where viruses can be contracted and ways to prevent the spread."

The story of siblings Jess and Joe, who are on a mission to stop germs spreadingafter a tickle in Jess' throat turns into a giant cough and sneeze, also includes top tips for how families can prevent the spread at home, a picture guide on how to wash hands properly and a 'spot the germs' illustration to help youngsters identify where viruses can be picked up.

"Bye-Bye Germs is a relevant, up-to-date resource specifically produced to help educate early years children about how germs spread and why we need to wash our hands to prevent viruses like of coronavirus. We have combined our multidisciplinary knowledge to produce an educational resource that helps children to easily digest the science behind the story."

Dr Katie Laird, Head of Infectious Disease Research Group
and
Professor Sarah Younie, Professor in Education, Innovation and Technology
De Montford University, Leicester, United Kingdom.

Tips for parents and carers

This book follows the journey of germs that cause respiratory illnesses and what children can do to stop themselves, family and friends from getting ill.

The concepts covered by this book include what a germ is, germs being invisible to the naked eye and how they are transferred and cause illness.

When reading this book with children, use the tips and questions below to give you and the children a greater understanding of the science behind germs.

1)   What is a Germ? – Germs can either be a bacteria or a virus; the germs in this book are viruses. Bacteria (good and bad germs) are living and can multiply independently, both in us and on surfaces. Viruses must have a host (humans) to multiply and cause disease, they only survive on surfaces for short period of time (a few days). Cleaning surfaces and washing hands can remove bacteria AND viruses and keep us healthy. Bacteria can be treated with antibiotics, however, antibiotics don't work against viruses.

2)   Good Germs – Reassure children that not all germs are bad for you and that many germs are good, they help you digest your food, they are in children's favourite foods like cheese and yoghurt. Also, germs help children build up their immune systems to be strong and healthy.

3)   The Germs are Hiding – Explore with children the idea of germs hiding, so even though they can't see the germs, they ARE there and can make you poorly. Discuss how touching your face with your hands can transfer germs into your body via your mouth, nose and eyes and then make you poorly. Germs can get on your hands from coughing and sneezing on them. This is why it is so important for children to frequently wash their hands to remove the germs.

4)   The Germs are Gone – Although germs cause illness, they are easily removed from hands by washing with soap. Help children wash their hands with water, soap (bubbles, bubbles, bubbles), rinsing and drying to remove all the germs. This should be encouraged, particularly after coughing and sneezing into their hands, and always before eating meals. Ensure that the towels children use to dry their hands are clean and changed regularly, as towels harbour germs. Germs can be removed from surfaces such as toys by washing them using soapy water or a safe disinfectant spray.

By children catching coughs and sneezes in a tissue or in their elbow (if there is no tissue available) they are preventing their germs being passed on to friends and family. It is
important that the tissue is thrown in the bin to stop other surfaces becoming contaminated from it and clothes should be washed using the highest temperature the clothes allow with detergent.

5)   More Germs (Viruses) – Viruses replicate inside a human cell and use the tools of our cells to make more viruses, this can make us feel poorly. These viruses then go on to infect another person or contaminate a surface. It is important for children to understand that if they stop their germs being passed on to someone else, they stop others becoming poorly, and are therefore superheroes!

Jess and her brother Joe were playing with their toys when Jess felt a tickle in her throat.

The little tickle turned into a bigger tickle. And the bigger tickle turned into a giant cough and sneeze!

We shouldn't worry about germs too much, they are all around us. Some germs are friendly...

She carried on playing with Joe and their toys...

Jess must have passed her germs to Joe,
because next week, they felt very poorly
and stayed in bed.

The germs made Jess cough and sneeze, and Joe felt hot and shivery.

Then, Jess had an idea to

STOP THE GERMS!

She felt like a superhero.
She showed Joe how to wash
his hands properly.

Soap

Jess and Joe washed the naughty germs off their hands with soap.

Bye-bye germs - down the plug hole they go.

And now Jess and Joe have ...

...CLEAN HANDS

Clean hands means
NO GERMS.

If you feel a big tickle turning into a giant cough or a sneeze, you can be a superhero too...

Catch your sneeze or cough in a tissue...

Jess and Joe soon felt much better and were back playing with their toys and Mum.

Nobody wants the bad germs.

Keep your family healthy by washing your hands with soap. That way, your toys will be clean and you will be a...

HANDWASHING SUPERHERO!

SPOT THE GERMS!
There are TEN to find.

How do you wash your hands?

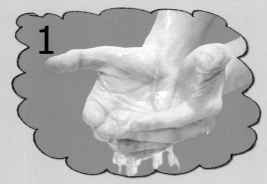

First wet your hands...

then apply soap.

Make sure your hands are soapy:

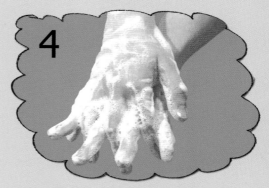

in between your fingers,

around your wrists

and in between your nails.

Then wash your hands with clean water.

Remember to wash for at least **20** seconds. That's as long as it takes to sing HAPPY BIRTHDAY TO YOU twice.

Questions and interaction

1. Do you know how a germ can make you poorly?

If you touch something with germs on and then put your hands in your mouth, the germs will make you poorly or if you breathe in someone else's coughs and sneezes.

2. Do you know how to make germs go away?

- Wash your hands with soap and then dry them
- Catch your coughs and sneezes in a tissue or in your elbow.

3. Why must you always catch your coughs and sneezes in a tissue or in your elbow?

If you catch the germs from your coughs and sneezes in a tissue and then throw it away, the germs are gone and not on your hand. If the germs go into your elbow make sure you wash those clothes! Catch your germs so you don't make your family and friends poorly.

4. Where do germs live?

Discuss with the child the kinds of places you can find germs, e.g. on toilets, on surfaces, in coughs and sneezes. Use the street scene in the book to explore this, as well as the game on the Germ's Journey website (www.germsjourney.com) to see where you can find germs and have fun uncovering their hiding places.

Dr Katie Laird is a Reader/Associate Professor in Microbiology in the School of Pharmacy, De Montfort University. She has a BSc (Hons) in Biology and obtained a PhD in applied microbiology in 2008. She is currently Head of the Infectious Disease Research group at DMU and has a team of researchers working on various projects.

Dr Laird's research is centred on the prevention of transmission of Healthcare Acquired Infections (HAIs) particularly on textiles and the development of novel antimicrobials as alternatives to current disinfectants and antibiotics.

Katie is passionate about science communication, which led her to co-found A Germ's Journey Educational Resources.

Sarah Younie is Professor of Education Innovation at De Montfort University and co-founder of the 'Education Futures Collaboration' charity. She has been involved in research for UNESCO, EU, UK government agencies, the BBC, local authorities and educational charities.

Sarah is an editor for the Learning to Teach book series and Editor-in-Chief for the international Journal of Technology, Pedagogy and Education. With 30 years teaching experience she continues to love teaching, with a passionate commitment to engaging learners of all ages.

Jules Marriner was a child in the 1970s, but has never let this hold her back. It was at University that she rediscovered her love of children's picture books and entered the Macmillan Children's Book prize.

Both author and illustrator of books such as Vincent and the Vampires, Royal Fleas and Nature Calls, she spends much of her time thinking up new and unconventional ideas.

Check out our other book about Germs!

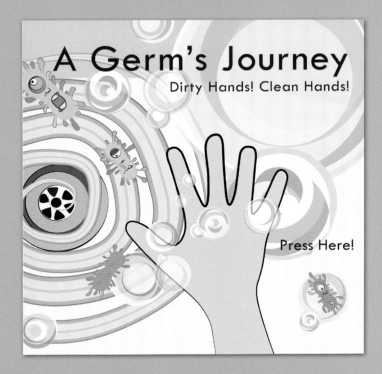

Follow a germ's journey – from the toilet seat to the tummy (and out again!)

This book explores the concepts of germs being invisible to the naked eye, multiplying and causing illness.

When children place their warm hands on the thermochromic patches, the multiplying germs are revealed.

The simple, bright and bold illustrations by Charlie Evans allow children to develop an understanding of science and health from a young age, while having fun in the process.

Written by Dr Katie Laird, Senior Lecturer in Microbiology in the De Montfort University School of Pharmacy, with Professor Sarah Younie and John Williams, A Germ's Journey is both educational and entertaining.

There is also an interactive website – www.germsjourney.com designed to reinforce the message and where children can play while learning the importance of hygiene.

Available from www.medinapublishing.com